Timeless Trails of the Yukon

Dolores Cline Brown

hancock
house

ISBN 0-88839-484-5

Cataloging in Publication Data
Brown, Dolores Cline,
    Timeless trails of the Yukon

ISBN 0-88839-484-5

1. Brown, Dolores Cline, 1918- 2. Hunting guides—Yukon
Territory—Biography. 3. Frontier and pioneer life—Yukon
Territory. 4. Yukon Territory—Biography. I. Title.
FC4023.1.B76 A3 2002   971.9'103'092   C2002-910145-X
F1093.B76A3 2002

Editor: Richard L. Rogers
Production: Vicki Duggan, Theodora Kobald
All photos courtesy of the author unless otherwise noted.

*We acknowledge the financial support of the Government of Canada through the
Book Publishing Industry Development Program for our publishing activities.*

Published simultaneously in Canada and the United States by

HANCOCK HOUSE PUBLISHERS LTD.
19313 Zero Avenue, Surrey, B.C. V3S 9R9
(604) 538-1114 Fax (604) 538-2262

HANCOCK HOUSE PUBLISHERS
1431 Harrison Avenue, Blaine, WA 98230-5005
(604) 538-1114 Fax (604) 538-2262
Web Site: www.hancockhouse.com email: sales@hancockhouse.com

Contents

To our staff of Indian guides, famous throughout the hunting world for their keen knowledge of the Northern bush, their courage and their fortitude.

Lonny Johnny	*John Kennedy*
Harry Baum	*Alec John*
Harry McGinty	*Gorden Mervyn*
Freddy Alfred	*Dinky Mervyn*
Alec Johnny	*Paul Germain*
Jimmy Johnny	*David Johnny*

The trails of the Yukon beckon to the soul weary of the pressures of civilization.

The far Northern wilderness trails lure those who love nature. They test one's courage and challenge one's weaknesses. The trails lead into the heart of God's creation and restore one's faith in the goodness of life and make one pause to delay time and age.

As the trails meander along azure blue lakes, across gushing glacial rivers and under the spell of rippling Northern lights, one is lifted into the glory of nature.

The lure of the trails must never be forgotten and the author invites her readers to share the grandeur and adventures of the Yukon Trails.

—DOLORES CLINE BROWN

Foreword

I have the French revolution to thank for my dream of going to Canada. An ancestor connected to the court of Louis XVI fled the guillotine by coming to French Prairie in Quebec. In time, his descendents migrated to Washington State, from where I eventually fled the hazards of civilization to the freedom of Canada.

The almost uninhabited Northern wilderness of the Yukon and I were made for each other. Its extremes of temperature complemented my extremes of temperament. Although I reveled in the raw frontier, I found it easier to adapt when it was toned down with a few French amenities. The howl of wolf packs in pursuit of some luckless prey seemed less intimidating when heard from my grandmother's cozy, four-poster canopy bed. When raging Arctic storms flung ice crystals against the windows, they seemed less formidable when hidden from view behind French boutique drapes. Rough plank floors lost their asperity covered with needlepoint rugs.

Not that I would ever think of giving up seeing the six-hour long migration of Barren Ground caribou, or watching a big grizzly flat on his back scooping blueberries into his mouth. Nor could I give up seeing the nimble angels of the white frosted peaks, the beautiful Dall sheep, nor the moose taking naps in our potato patch, nor the thrilling sight of the long noisy Vs of wild Canadian honkers loudly announcing their annual departure from the Yukon and, just as cacophonously, their return.

One must remember my dream was late in its consummation. I was born and raised in cities, so the last frontier seemed frightingly intimidating. But it was worth the seventeen close encounters I had with grizzlies, the seventy below temperatures and, best of all, meeting and knowing the true Frontier men of the North, now vanishing into the legends of history.

No one could express my love for the North better than that grand old poet laureate Robert Service when he wrote "Me For The Yukon, YIPPEE!"

Vive Valeque

Chapter 1

BEYOND DREAMS

Its Capital complex is the soul and pride of Washington State and justifiably famous as the most beautiful of all the State Capitals. Its luxurious landscaped grounds, with their sunken gardens featuring various varieties of exotic roses, fountains spraying colored rainbows, and sidewalks edged with Japanese cherry trees whose pink and white blossoms fill the spring air with delightful fragrances, make the spirit soar.

Serving as secretary to the Capital's brilliant economist, Dr. J.A. McKibbin, could have been rewarding work but for the fact I had inherited restless genes from two early pioneering ancestors; Great Grandmother was born in a covered wagon on the old Oregon Trail near Canby Oregon, while my great, great Grandfather, a French aristocrat attending Louis XVI, had escaped the guillotine with only the family jewels (an exquisite garnet necklace I eventually inherited) and fled to French Prairie to pioneer in Quebec, Canada.

Their diaries of exciting adventures had been handed down as family treasures and reading them left me longing for the more basic, self-reliant life of a pioneer. But the old covered wagon trails were now under super busy highways, the wide open spaces crowded with suburbs and cities, the glare of harsh electric lights had overwhelmed the soft glow of lamp and candle light, and picturesque log cabins were superseded by lumber houses. Sadly, I realized I had been born a hundred years too late to be a bona fide pioneer.

Desperate to escape the stress of a high-tech society, I decided to visit Mrs. Walt Disney in California. Maybe she would know of some place in need of pioneering. Before her marriage to Walt, she was Lillian Bounds, who lived with her family next door to my Aunt Fannie and Uncle John Bramlett on the Nez Perce Indian reservation in Lapwai, Idaho. She and her sister, Blanch, always gravitated to Aunt Fannie's kitchen when she was baking her famous plump, raisin-filled cookies. Later my sister, Fleta Mae, and Lillian, enamored by Lilly Dache and Princess Eugenie hats, took a millinery course together in Lewiston, Idaho. After Lillian married Walt and moved to California, she invited family members from time to time to visit and she never forgot my aunt's cookies.

Intending to surprise Lillian, I arrived in Los Angeles only to find Lillian had taken a trip with Walt. Smog obliterated the city and traffic was so heavy, it was unbelievable that California ever needed pioneering.

Back in Olympia I could only imagine some day owning a horse to ride the park bridle paths with a dog for companionship. To ease my heart aching with the need to flee modern stress and live a more simple life, I found solace in the great naturalists of the day — John Muir, Enos Mills, Steven Graham. When one wrote:

"One everlasting whisper day and night repeated so; Something hidden go and find it; go and look behind the ranges. Something lost behind the ranges, lost and waiting for you. GO."

But where would I go? Such advice sent me tossing on my pillows and night after night I wondered, was there really something wonderful waiting for me? If so, where? One sleeplessly tossing night I heard in the dark skies the migrating cries of wild geese flying North. I suddenly realized in going to California, I had gone South, the wrong direction. I decided that on my next vacation I was going to follow the wild geese North. My book Yukon Trophy Trails gives a full account of that trip, where I met the man of my dreams, a real pioneer, a famous big game outfitter and guide in the Yukon. We were married in the historical log church in Whitehorse. Just as the naturalist said, he was waiting for me to share his pioneer life.

I didn't fully realize I was pioneering until I was doing our laundry in a tub on a washboard, carrying water from a bubbly spring, cooking on fragrant wood burning stove, reading by soft kerosene lamps and being intimidated by the outhouse at fifty below.

Moving North of the 60th parallel plummeted me into a whole new world that exuded mystery and magic. Surrounding me were thousands of miles of unpopulated wilderness where the sun shone brightly at midnight, the Northern Lights dazzled in winter, where there were seven months of snow and ice, an abundance of wild game, and lakes and streams glutted with fish.

I was to find the Yukon to be a celebration of survival. The very word YUKON strikes a cord of awe. Is it the thrill of some dim, prehistoric memory when nature flung a challenge to man, testing his right to life, measuring his endurance, molding into him strength of body, keenness of mind and determination of spirit?

Is it some haunting memory that fades into only a feeling? A feeling which cannot be interpreted, of some stupendous past when tremendous odds were faced; the feared mammoths of the glacier age, the bone chilling cold, treacherous river crossings, gnawing hunger, the fight to survive or fade into memory. I was determined to survive.

As a big game outfitter, my husband's clients came from all over the world to hunt the white angels of glaciated peaks, the Dall sheep, the caribou that migrate by the thousands, the feared grizzly bear and the largest of the ruminates, the moose.

Louis and his staff of full-blooded Indian guides of the NaCho Nyak Dun tribe took on the task of turning an American secretary into a Canadian big game guide. These Indians have survived for thousands of years in one of the most remote and hostile places on earth, making them superb outdoorsmen. They were my teachers. To say our diverse cultures baffled both of us would be an understatement. It was their determination to teach me the self-control that ensured I'm alive today. Their methods would sometimes send me into a rage. If a horse stepped on my foot I wanted to yell, if the packtrain stirred up a hornets nest and they stung me I wanted to cry, but the guides would hop around, screeching outlandishly until I shut up. No matter how close a grizzly came to me I was to stand my ground and never, never run. They ground it into me — whatever happened I was to remain calm. It was this lesson that enabled me to remain still while a grizzly stood twelve feet away looking me over until he decided I wasn't interesting and crashed off into the underbrush. Having learned it, I survived the time a grizzly spent the night trying to knock down the stilt cache I was on while I read my little book of Emerson Essays until dawn, when it was light enough to see the iron sights of my 270 Winchester. By staying calm, I was able to make the fatal shot. Had I not been taught to control my fears I'm sure I would have worked myself into such a state of nerves I wouldn't have been able to hit the broadside of a barn. Because the guides taught me how to handle tight situations, I have been able to survive seventeen close grizzly encounters and three grizzly charges, which really tests the nerves.

After gaining toughness on the trail, I had the energy to study the flora we rode through. I found many botanical treasures in the vast remote valleys. One year I took pictures of fifty-four varieties of wild flowers. On one mountain, there grows a species of plant that is unique in the world to that single rocky slope. The Editors of Alaska Yukon Flower Guide state: "The territory is so vast and so much of it literal-

8

ly unexplored by botanists, that it is entirely possible that species hitherto unknown may be discovered in years to come."

In the high country of our hunting area of the Bonnet Plume, Wind and Snake rivers there is no summer, only spring, fall and winter, making the growing season very short. The lakes do not lose their crystal icing until July, when fishing is fabulous. The hunters always enjoyed fried trout for breakfast served with hot baking powder biscuits and wild blueberry jam, the berries picked when riding through hundreds of acres of blueberry bushes.

At times we were able to serve our guests delicious salads made of wild celery, wild carrots, lettuce and bear roots. Even medicinal plants were taught me by our chief guide, Lonny Johnny, a Ft. Mackenzie Indian who was once a medicine man.

I detested the rough clothes I had to wear to withstand the rigors of the hunting trails, so at night I indulged my love of finer raiment by rolling into my sleeping bag wearing lace trimmed silk nightgowns brother Frank sent me from Paris.

Because of the muskeg on the hunt, I had to wear rubber and leather shoepacks. In the winter, because of the snow and cold, I had to wear moose skin mucklucks. They both gave my feet more freedom and extended my shoe size from 4AA to 7C and I was no longer able to wear the forty-two pair of shoes I had brought from the States.

We became so well known internationally that we were unable to accommodate all those who wished to book a hunt with us. As a result, the Canadian Government issued me a license to hunt a large area in the Mt. Ortel and Lancing district, making me the first woman in the Yukon to be a big game outfitter.

I booked mostly big game hunters from Switzerland for several reasons. They had such a deep appreciation and love for our vast wilderness, they were wonderful sportsmen, respected the guides' skill, were excellent shots and, not least of all, they brought me large tooled leather boxes of Swiss chocolates.

Perhaps the most remarkable hunt was when Ernest Hemmingway's brother-in-law took an extremely large caribou with a double shovel that won Mr. Miller a place in the Boone and Crocket trophy book of records.

One of my favorite hunters was Helen Nobholts, owner of one of the largest outdoor clothing companies in Europe. She brought her own taxidermist for she had acquired extra tags to collect for a museum. She shot the largest moose that was ever taken on any of our hunts and had it fully mounted. It is now on display in Salzburg.

Surprisingly, some of the younger hunters were not physically up to the hardships of the trophy trails but some of the elderly were tough enough to withstand any hardships. I remember one hunter's letters sounded as if he was a hardened prizefighter. When he arrived he was hobbling with a cane and had passed his ninetieth birthday. Had the plane not departed I would have sent him back. He was determined to have another hunt. Although he couldn't walk, he could certainly ride, having been in the horse marines in China.

The hardship and danger on the trophy trail either make one or break one. The cheerfulness and endurance of my husband and his guides under the most difficult conditions spurred me to never let them down. I carry many physical scars. I have been accidentally shot by an excited hunter, had a hole punched in my eye by brush, twice broken an ankle, suffered a bout of pneumonia while riding the trails with a temperature of a hundred and three. I have no regrets. The Yukon has restored my health, given me a deep appreciation for nature, taught me full responsibility for my own actions, and, best of all, given me the love of a man who was once only a dream.

I look back to my Olympia days when I so wanted a horse. Now I have forty horses. When I so wanted a dog, now I have a team of eight huskies. When I wanted a log cabin, now I have four. When I dreamed of having a companion, now I have a wonderful husband.

We live a happy pioneer life without the modern amenities civilization deems so important. Living close to nature endows us with life's realities. Wild life insists on sharing our life.

Wolves come into the garden to dig up the fish fertilizer. Fox hunt for mice in the flowerbeds. Moose find the potato patch a good place to take a nap. Now and then, grizzly bears come to check out the place or dig for parka squirrels. Otters slide down the bank to splash in our water hole. Grouse scratch on the roof for needed gravel. Owls plug up the stovepipe. Thousands of wild ducks and geese come to feed along the lakeshore below the cabin before starting on their migration. They all make life fascinating. I am often reminded of a song "If you don't have a dream, how you gonna have a dream come true?"

With all my heart I know any woman who refuses to be bluffed by her fears and supports her courage can make her dream come true. Your dream is God guiding you to a better Life. Happy dreaming.

Chapter 2

PIONEERING
NORTH OF 60

Only love could have given me the courage to pack my sterling silver and French antique furniture in my lovely apartment overlooking the sunken rose gardens of Washington's State Capital, where I was a secretary, and unpack in a log cabin North of 60 in the shadow of the Arctic Circle.

I was determined nothing was going to extirpate my passion to pioneer. It was in my blood. My pregnant great-great grandmother had traveled across the continent in a covered wagon and delivered my great grandmother on the Oregon Trail just east of Canby, Oregon, while the wagon train circled to prepare for an Indian attack.

My maternal grandmother pioneered by marrying a frontier doctor and managed to survive without television or computers and a host of other necessities not yet invented.

The Yukon had everything a pioneer could pray for — lack of roads, scarcity of people, two hundred and seven thousand square miles of untarnished wilderness! This was ideal for my venture into pioneering and Louis's guiding business.

My brand new husband grew alarmed when unloading the two tons of my possessions which I considered essential for refining the rough edges of pioneering and which he considered incongruous for the frontier Northern wilderness. Some of his fears were substantiated when his eighteen by twenty-foot bachelor's cabin couldn't even hold half the load. I grew apoplectic realizing great grandmother's fragile Louis XV chair that had made it over the old Oregon Trail could never make it through seven winter months on a snow bank.

Louis quickly sized up the situation and announced a larger cabin had to be built before old man winter plummeted temperatures down to 70 or 80 below Fahrenheit. I was aghast. The Yukon could get as cold as Siberia!

I faced the first reality of pioneering. It came as a shock when Louis shouldered an axe and headed for the forest of Arctic spruce to procure building material for our new home, without first buying the land. My husband explained the land was free, and there was no need for a contractor, plumber, or electrician, since we were on our own. As for a mortgage, he had enough money to buy the nails, but there was need for an architect so he suggested, "You better get busy and draw up a plan so I'll know how many logs to cut."

Long ago I had decided a home of my very own must be like grandmother's spacious old Victorian house, but without the wrap around porch and ginger bread trim. The interior, so dear to my childhood, must be the same. Carefully I drew the spacious foyer with its elegant winding stairs leading up to four commodious bedrooms from which had once descended many a corseted and bustled bride to make a grand entrance into the bay windowed parlor, connected to the living-room by a high arch, from which had hung, according to the occasion, wedding bells or mistletoe. Double French doors lead to the dining room with seating capacity to accommodate a regiment of relatives for reunions. A butler's pantry, kitchen, breakfast nook, two bedrooms, bathrooms, halls, closets, and laundry room completed the plan.

That glorious house had no historical status, because no famous dignitary ever slept there. However, grandfather did, which should have given it a ten-star rating. He was the most sought after man in Columbia County. Early settlers rushed their bullet wounds, knife cuts, liver complaints, tummy aches or anything else that plagues the human anatomy to old Doc Andrus. He delivered most of the population of Dayton, Washington. My five aunts recruited their husbands from grandfather's recuperating patients. As a pioneering doctor, he saved many lives. As a moonlighting vigilante, he helped hang a few.

I had just finished adding on the back porch, completing the plan when Louis returned, smelling deliciously of fragrant spruce pitch and oozing sweat. I excitedly showed him the rough draft for our first very own home. There was a deafening silence. Mustering all his will power to remain calm, he tensely explained that anyone born and raised in cities had lost their connection with reality. Furthermore, at seventy below, he would have to clear cut most of the Arctic spruce in the region to heat a sixteen-room house. As he warmed to the subject, he grew eloquently inspired. Since we were to have no electricity, stairs were boobytraps for kerosene lamps. Stumbling up or down stairs, the lamp would be dropped, explode and burn the cabin down.

Furthermore, few people had the fortitude to bump over an old bush road, paddle a canoe across the wide expanse of the mighty Stewart River and hike a mile over a caribou trail in heavily populated grizzly country to visit us, thus the four bedrooms could be eliminated. When Louis caught his breath, he consolidated the parlor, living- room, dining room, and kitchen into one room. Next went the butler's pantry. My sterling silver could be polished in the kitchen. The bedrooms could wait their fate until we counted the logs. The outhouse would replace the bathrooms.

At that point, I felt like taking the axe and I wasn't heading for the timber.

To keep me from percolating any more outlandish ideas, Louis handed me a two-handle drawing knife to peel bark from the trees as he felled them. It was the toughest job I had ever tackled. In her diaries, great grandmother never mentioned the backbreaking, muscle torturing, finger blistering, sticky job of peeling logs. She had only extolled the beauty of the campfire as she heated the fluted flat irons to iron the six petticoats she wore daily.

Not until most of my fingers were bandaged did we have enough logs to start building. It took the combined effort of two horses, Louis and my feeble strength to get the walls up. When the top beams were in place, we had roof and floor problems. Early Hudson Bay fur traders and trappers used small poplar poles for the ceiling and roof, topping them with moss and dirt. Larger poles made a convenient floor that let the dirt fall between the cracks, meaning no sweeping was required. I doubted the slender legs of my French antique chairs would be able to negotiate the cracks.

Fortunately, a small Bell saw mill Louis had ordered three years previously arrived unexpectedly. While Louis sawed lumber for the roof and floor, I gathered tons of moss to plug up the cracks between the logs to keep the icy winds from the Barrens, called the death fog, from refrigerating the interior.

When early frosts tinted the mountainsides with a brilliant display of fiery red Delacroix and glowing orange shades of Rubens we grew desperate for windows. The Yukon had run out of glass windows. The old trappers used flour sacks but that was out of the question. I wanted a clear view looking out to spot any trespassing wolves or grizzly. An August snow storm refreshed Louis's memory. An old roadhouse used during the Klondike Gold Rush might still have windows. We drove the seventy miles over rutted dirt roads and were animated with joy when we saw the sun glistening on enough bubbly glass windows to thwart the icy winds of the Arctic.

My keen disappointment over not having those glorious, impressive stairs had worried Louis, and he had this in mind when he suggested having a massive rock fireplace, emphasizing it would be even more impressive and much more practical than stairs.

With this project in mind, we headed for Dawson City, the famous gold rush town that now looked as if it was on one big bender with its frost heaved houses tilting in every direction. We drove on through, heading for Bonanza Creek where mammoth gold dredges had left hill size piles of white quartz rocks. We loaded enough quartz for our fireplace and for months we had this rock pile in our living quarters while Louis struggled to get the chimney high enough to go through the roof. Relatives had sent chemically treated rolls of paper to celebrate its completion with a blaze of colored flames. At long last, the final rock was in place. The great day had arrived. Reading from great grandmother's diary, we had spent a fortune buying a black cast iron kettle that now rested full of moose meat on the kindling wood. Henceforth, like my pioneering ancestor, we would be eating our meals cooked on a campfire. With great expectation of gratification for his hard labour, Louis struck the match. Big clouds of black smoke billowed out into the room. We raced to open doors and windows while I fervently wished he had built the stairs instead. Louis was devastated, tears glistened in his eyes as he wondered what he had done wrong. Seeing my dear husband so disappointed over his effort to replace my beloved stairs gave me an idea. "Dear, is the damper open?"

Sheepishly, he flipped open the damper and soon green, blue, yellow, and red flames licked the white quartz rocks and highlighted the honey toned log walls. The moose stew began bubbling in the pot and I vowed I would never mention stairs again.

I realized too late that in university I should have taken fewer art and ancient languages and instead taken a full course in architecture. As any good architect would do, I would have studied the possibility of unexpected complications to avoid them. However, I didn't and when the unexpected happened, it was a shock. One day, while I was frying moose steaks, a grizzly ambled up and looked through the window to check out a meal. It became frighteningly clear there should have been fewer windows located higher up on the walls.

But would an architect have studied the Northern habitat enough to know that in the Yukon there are a lot of uncaged animals running wild and a pack of wolves would visit our huskies just twenty feet from the back door, and then designed a wolf-proof porch to enclose the door?

Perhaps the most extensive alteration needed was to the roof. To the delight of the pintail grouse, the deep, dark earth first appears in early spring around the chimney on our roof. Badly in need of gravel to grind the food in their gizzards, they energetically scratch, sending down a sandstorm on the canopy of the four-poster bed.

I would hate to give up the dirt roof now as it makes an ideal flowerbed to raise a gorgeous array of annuals, reminders of home. Below, wild flowers such as lupins, chiming bells, crocuses, and wild roses bloom in abundance.

Grandmother Nancy would have loved our home, but I often wonder how she would react to seeing her cherished four-poster canopy bed and her solid maple escritoire ensconced between logs. In a way, she has helped me pioneer, for without some of her treasures to soften the rough edges of a Northern frontier, the life might have been more than I had bargained for. However, with her silver tea set to make a quick comforting cup of tea when the wolf packs vocalize their hunting, pioneering is great.

Chapter 3

RUFFLES ON MY PANTS

My husband kicked open the cabin door, carried me through and dumped me on the bed. Hurriedly taking off my boots, he anxiously examined my feet, while tears gushed through my frozen eyelashes. I had never been so cold in my life. Louis let out a deep sigh of relief, "Well, your damn lucky your feet aren't frozen, but they should be, wearing those fool boots. I told you they weren't fit for the Yukon."

I gave my boots a reproachful look. They were beautiful. Made of burgundy red suede, with blue fox fur ankle cuffs and only a two and a quarter inch heel. They were purchased as a part of my survival gear for the sub Arctic. I glared at my husband, "That salesman said they were good for fifty below."

"FIFTY BELOW," my husband roared. "Its only thirty below now and had we hiked another mile you'd have to have your feet cut off. Those fool southern salesman should be shot for telling you such a damn lie."

Louis banged out the door, returning with a pair of mukluks and a red fox skin. He unsheathed his hunting knife, cut the fox skin in two, stuffed each half into a mukluk, and jammed my feet into them. "Now this is the kind of foot gear you need. These will have to do until I can take you down to the Indian village and have the Indians make you a pair of mukluks that will fit over two pair of heavy wool Cowichin socks and a pair of thick felt liners."

I let out a wail: "It makes me look club footed."

"You want to keep your feet don't you?"

"Could the Indians put heels on the mukluks?"

"Good God, NO!"

"Just a little heel?"

"How in hell are you going to snowshoe in heels? Why do you want those ridiculous heels anyway?"

I wasn't about to tell my husband, but the truth was that only by wearing spike heels could I be five feet tall. I hated being short and wearing high heels for so long had so shrunk the tendons in my legs that it nearly killed me to go flat-footed. It began to dawn on me, maybe the Far North was going to change my life drastically.

Before coming to the Yukon to marry a Canadian big game outfitter and guide, I didn't know what was going to be needed in such a cold climate. I did know the salary I earned as a secretary at the Washington State Capitol could never be stretched to replace a wardrobe for a temperate zone, or a whole new wardrobe for a zero zone. It would bankrupt me.

In my dilemma, I called my brother, who had just returned from his home in Arosa, Switzerland, to his home in Hollywood. I sobbed out my woes, I knew tears would have better luck with Frank.

"Frank dear, I can't go North without a lot of new clothes and I don't have that much money."

"Maybe you'll change your mind about going."

"And be an old maid? NEVER!"

"Well, what do you need?"

"Since I'm marrying a big game guide I'll be riding a horse."

"Surely you have pants you can wear?"

"No, I hate pants."

"Sis, you're crazy, all women are wearing pants."

"Don't I know it. Stretched over a lot of fat fannies."

"Like it or not, you're going to have to wear them. I'll be in New York next week. I'll buy you a couple of riding outfits while I'm there."

"And Frank, I'll need other things."

"What?"

"Shoes."

"You always did have trouble buying shoes."

"That's because I wear size four, double A width."

"You have trouble buying them in Olympia, so you'll never get that size on a northern frontier."

"The Yukon has seven months of winter so I must have shoes."

"Tell you what. Fly down here. I know of a place that specializes in small shoes."

Therefore, I flew down to Hollywood. Frank and I shopped for shoes at a small Jewish store the next street over from Hollywood and Vine. They sold show case shoes that other, more elite stores like I. Magnums, couldn't sell. Such stores only displayed them in their windows because they were so small and cute. Sort of a physiological scheme to tempt in women with big feet.

Frank never did things by halves. He had ushered in my thirteenth birthday by taking some of my gawky, braced toothed friends and me to the Tracadaro. I was too embarrassed to enjoy the party because all the showgirls wore were big-feathered war bonnets and G-strings. Now, since he was my big brother and suffered from the misconception that he had more grey matter, he took full charge. He kept two salesmen running as if he were a sergeant of the Marines. No one really knew what was needed for the North. No matter how high the heel, if my toes were encased, the shoes were considered sturdy enough for North of the 60th parallel.

That is why I landed in the Yukon with forty-two pairs of shoes. Frank wanted to make sure his little sister wouldn't run out of shoes and have to wade through snow bare-footed. Most of the heels eventually became permanently stuck in the cracks of the board sidewalks of Mayo and Dawson City.

Several packages had come from I. Millers of New York. That is why I rode a horse through thick brush and snagging willows while wearing English broadcloth riding britches and waded through murky muskeg in polished English riding boots.

When I started out on the big game trails of the Wind and Bonnet Plume rivers, I looked more like I was heading for England's Royal Ascot than heading for a hunt in some of the wildest, most remote and rugged country on the continent. As if I was insulting masculine prerogatives, Mother Nature assaulted my clothes with a vengeance.

First, a playful arctic spruce jerked my black velvet cap off my head and dropped it onto the muskeg to be pounded by the whole pack string. A passing caribou horn ripped my jacket from North to South as it was carried on a top pack by old Queeny. My britches were overly ventilated by sparks from a crackling campfire. My extra bag of clothes, carried by Tootsie, was bucked off in the middle of the Bonnet Plume River. They dried out fine over a campfire, but shrank until a five-year-old couldn't get into them. When sloshing through a valley of nigger heads, the soles of my riding boots parted from the tops.

My six-foot husband came to the rescue and offered to share some of his clothes. He had to, because I was going around with too much exposed. I never before realized how much my husband's shape differed from mine. Where he concaved, I convexed. His high altitude also caused problems. We had no scissors to scale things down to my height, so a skinning knife was used to make alterations. It was a success until

18

I got hold of the wrong pair of chaps and, to Louis's horror and dismay, cut a foot off of his best concho studded chaparaios.

As soon as the hunt was over, I plunged back into dresses, only to eventually discover mosquitoes and horse flies found the wide open spaces of skirts a good hunting ground for a meal. In winter, the air circulated too many Ice crystals up, encircling a tender gluteus maximus and froze my bottom. It was pants or death, so back to pants, but with a whole new couturier flair.

Since God had made me a female, I was going to remain feminine. I refused to be stuck with fly front jeans, stone washed jeans, or any other kind of Jeans, which were an affront to good looking legs. I fought like Sugar Ray Robinson to hang onto my silky sheer panty hose. The day battalion after battalion of mosquitoes attacked, even Sugar would have capitulated. Although my legs were not in the same class as Marlene Dietrich's famous gams, still they were good enough to wear clocked hose and ankle bracelets and now they had to become hidden assets.

Not to be totally defeated, I made a pair of pants with legs six times wider than Jeans with two rows of contrasting ruffles edging the bottom. The matching top with a yoke of ruffles made a very fetching outfit. If not a Dior or Chanel creation, it was at least a feminine victory over fly fronts.

Proud of my new outfit I pranced in front of my husband, expecting "ooos" and "ahs" of admiration. He ignored me.

"Get ready, we are going to town."

"I'm ready."

In unbelieving horror Louis stammered "I...I..n..n th..th...that?"

"Why not?"

"Not with me. If you fell out of the canoe and all those bottom rags got soaked you'd sink and drown."

At home every time the ruffles swished past those worn Levis Louis remained stolid, but he could sure react to tight jeans.

After fifty below zero, I became a fur-bearing animal with fur parka, fur mitts, and fur mukluks. Swathed in muskrat, beaver, lynx, and blue fox, I was in seventh heaven. Fur is so luxuriously rich and soft and, most important when your steamy breath crackles into icy crystals, it can keep you from freezing to death. I was lucky to be married to the best fur trapper in the Yukon. It takes eighty-two below zero to fully appreciate his skill.

Along with the belief that all people of the Yukon live in igloos, those south of the border have the idea that as soon as you are isolated from the outside world you deteriorate. When I invited two of my close friends for a visit, I waited to sharpen my knife over their rejections.

Jeanie must have been laughing with unrestrained mirth when she wrote: "Dolores, I'd rather remember you as you were. After six months in that God forsaken frozen place you'll be going around in an old faded kimono, run over carpet slippers and your hair stringing over your eyes."

In retaliation I blitzed them with pictures of my elegant and luxurious fur parkas and when I ran out of my own, I borrowed others to make them so green with envy they were moaning over their cloth-coated poverty.

My introduction to Northern society was a New Year dance in Warrens log hall. Naturally, I dressed the same as I did when going to a club dance in Olympia — a low cut, strapless evening gown, and rhinestone-studded French heels.

On arrival, I felt a little exposed because all the other women wore necklines to their jaws and sleeves to their thumbs. Peeping from under their floor length evening gowns were beaded, moose-skin mukluks. I didn't have long to puzzle over this Northern style because after dancing with the seventh heavy, scratchy wool shirt I broke out in fiery red bumps all across my white bosom. When the wool shirts got to steaming, they opened the front and back doors to let in fifty below breezes to circulate. Within minutes my feet were too numb to dance, but the mukluks kept skipping over the splintered floor.

The North changed me in many ways. After years of wearing mukluks in the winter and heavy shoepacks in the summer, my feet grew from size 4 AA to 7CC. For the first time I had warm feet because the Northern footwear allowed all the little red corpuscles to circulate, where before they were damned up in tight shoes. Still, given a choice, I would rather have cold feet and small underpins.

The first winter I had a glorious glutinous good time eating fat caribou, fat moose, and fat snowshoe rabbits. Spring came as a shock when I tried to dress for town in my last year's clothes. My town clothes got stuck in the middle of my anatomy. Never again would I weigh a hundred and five pounds.

Dr. Alexis Carrol, a surgeon and scientist famous for his book Man the Unknown thinks the Far North is the ideal place for man to develop physically, mentally and spiritually.

Which means, the North challenges your brain to think and face reality. No brains, No survival. I survived.

Chapter 4

YUKON WOWS GUESTS

Any relation to my first guest to the Yukon is purely coincidental. It would be to embarrassing for both to acknowledge any degree of kinship. She that there existed a Northern barbarian on the family tree. I of being related to anyone who screeched at a little old bear.

I soon learned visiting guests react to the Yukon in much the same manner as a person taking a newly discovered wonder drug. The side effects can be either tranquilizing or terrifying.

Some are all for giving the Yukon back to the ice age, others could tolerate it if a string of Royal Hilton's were built across the muskeg. Hardier souls think it would be God's country if it were heated.

After spending two months vacationing in the South, Margo flew from Miami's Hilton hotel to Dawson City's Pearl Harbour hotel. She was not impressed. In fact, she had a seizure at the sight of water stained wallpaper in her hotel room. I thought it gave a romantic touch of the good old 1898 days of the Klondike gold rush.

After leaving her French heels in the cracks of Dawson's board sidewalks while her powder blue suit collected clouds of dust from the unpaved streets, we headed for home. A hundred and twenty-five miles through unpopulated wilderness. She thought the Tombstone Mountains were aptly named. Passing Gravel Lake, she thought any country that could produce a snowstorm in August was headed for the glacier age and with good riddance. I shuddered. What would be her reaction to our hand-hewn log cabin with its massive rock fireplace standing between the kitchen and living room like an Aku Aku statue, a sentinel over all our activities?

Suddenly with a shriek, Margo grabbed me around the neck and we headed for a gully. A mother Cross fox and her three playful kits were out hunting for lunch. Margo mistook them to be prowling jaguars.

Fearing another onslaught, we barely crawled past ten miles of blueberry bushes known to be frequented by grizzly.

We were coasting past Barlow Lake when I slammed on the brakes at the sight of a dark object in the middle of the road. A cow moose was struggling to her feet, leaving a wet, squirming, newborn calf. Mamma Moose's hackles rose and she charged. From my small English Anglia, she looked as terrifying as an oncoming freight train. With a loud yelp, Margo fell out the car door, sprinting up the road with mamma right behind her. Backing up at full speed, I drove between them, expecting mamma to straddle the car at any moment. Her baby struggled to its feet and bleated. Mamma slid to a stop, hesitated, turned, and trotted back to her offspring, leading it off the road into thick brush.

Pleading with Margo, I explained that the moose was only bluffing, that had she been mean, we would be gored by now, and that she was just a loving mother moose, fearful for her baby. Reluctantly Margo climbed back into the car. Every few moments, at Margo's insistence, I blasted the horn to clear the road of any wildlife that might challenge our right to travel the highway.

Margo showed intense relief to be within four solid log walls of our cabin. She asked with concern if any rocks ever fell from our fireplace. My husband, Louis, assured her he had personally glued them firmly together with a strong mix of cement and it would take an earthquake the magnitude of Krakatoa to dislodge them.

However, it wasn't until she was shown the guestroom, with its four poster bed with ball fringed canopy, that she felt she was in some semblance of civilization.

Back in the living room, I was serving tea while Louis was expounding on the soothing, peaceful and relaxing atmosphere of the Yukon when an ominous dark shadow blotted out the sunlight. A black bear was nonchalantly strolling past the window. With a shriek, Margo disappeared as Louis and I grabbed our guns and took after the bear. The bear ran down the bank and into thick timber before we could get in a shot.

Returning to the cabin, we couldn't open the door. Exasperated Louis swore. "The damn door's stuck."

He was preparing to ram the door, when I yelled, "STOP", I knew if those size 44 shoulders hit the door with full force, all twelve panes of the glass I had labored so hard to putty in would fly out and shatter on the cement steps.

I fiddled with the doorknob "I think the key has been turned."

"What ever for?" Louis asked incredulously.

"To lock the bear out."

"WHAT!!?"

"Dear, why don't you do your chores, while I get the door unlocked."

I ran to the guest bedroom window. Peering in I saw a hump of covers in the middle of the bed. The ball fringe on the bed's canopy was jerking spasmodically.

"Margo, the bear is gone, everything is safe. That was just a little bear!"

A beautiful coifed head surfaced, "LITTLE MY FOOT. That was a BIG bear and I've seen hundreds in the zoo's."

"Well, he's gone and ..."

"He'll be back."

"Of course he will."

"Why, for heavens sake?"

"We built on his trail."

"You WHAT?"

"Dear, if you'll unlock the door, I'll...."

"If you'll promise to take me to the plane today so I can fly back to New York, I'll unlock the door. The Yukon has to many beasts running loose, scaring hell out of people. They should be caged. Promise to take me to the plane?"

"Promise? I'll GUARANTEE it."

Our next guest was proceeded by a two foot by four foot wooden box, plastered with foreign stamps. Excitedly prying off the lid, I became paralyzed with awe. Nestling in fluffs of pink tissue paper was an exquisite eighteen inch doll, made just for me, so said the tag. Dressed in pink-sashed, white crepe-de-chine hoop skirted dress and wearing a Parisian hat trimmed with pink silk roses, sweeping ostrich plumes and clouds of tulle, she was breathlessly beautiful, a dream of elegance. And just think, to this raw frontier wilderness had come this gorgeous creation!

Louis hovering near, said "There's more gifts."

From a froth of tissue paper Louis lifted out a Dresden figurine, dated 1760. A girl in frill lace, sat on a sofa petting her Russian wolf hound. A masterpiece of art.

I was almost overcome with rapture when Louis handed me yet another gift. A tooled leather box of Swiss chocolates. Popping a cognac-centred candy in my mouth and savoring the delicate sweet-

23

ness as it melted over my tongue, I vowed that everything had to be perfect for Dr. Weber's visit from Switzerland.

Preparations for his arrival reached fever pitch. Everything had to be faultless, the cabin spotless, food of gourmet quality, my dress new, and my hair coiffured in the latest.

Louis had been after me for weeks to clean out the chicken house. Even the chickens were to appear at their best for Dr. Weber.

Donning a pair of torn jeans and hurriedly tying a rag around my head, I vigorously attacked the job until I heard the soft purr of a motor. Sticking my head out of the chicken coup, I saw a large, chauffeured Cadillac gliding smoothly into the yard. Wildly thinking of committing suicide, climbing a tree or just fainting, I braced myself, trying to simulate nonchalance. With shaking knees I went to face the polished, dignified and suave personage of Dr. Weber stepping out of the limousine, the door held open by his valet.

Jerking the rag from my uncoiffed head, clutching a hand over the tear in my pants, I stretched my mouth into what I hoped was a decorous smile of welcome.

Dr. Weber, gave me a startled look. MY GOD, was he thinking, did I send those expensive gifts to that uncouth creature? However, Dr. Weber didn't own a string of stores across Europe and speak seven different languages without having a keen perception. His eyes began to twinkle when he saw my cool dignity was a farce and that underneath I was embarrassed to death.

The chauffeur, loaded down with Jetliner luggage, interrupted my floundering greeting by asking directions to Dr. Weber's suit of rooms.

Heading the procession, I guided them around a tub of soapy scrub water to the guest room, where the four poster bed stood nude. I hadn't had time to place the freshly laundered canopy cover back on the frame, which was just as well, as the valet used the over head slats to hang some of Dr. Weber's lounging apparel.

Dr. Weber had come to hunt moose. He had emphatically stated in his letters that he would not sleep in a tent, so Louis had obtained a permit to hunt from the ranch. Each night they would return to sleep in the safety of our log cabin. This man of fortune wanted to avoid any danger. Unfortunately, he had read one of my published articles describing a grizzly ripping up our tents. On meeting Louis he said: "No grizzly Louis, just moose, just moose."

At six o'clock the next morning, Louis brought two saddled horses to the cabin, ready to start hunting. Dr. Weber hadn't shown up yet.

24

When his valet came from the bunk house, I gave him a breakfast tray for his master. Immediately the valet returned with the tray untouched, followed by Dr. Weber in his lounging robe.

Because the large rock fireplace is the centre piece of our kitchen, a cheerful log fire was burning. Dr. Weber with suave courtesy declined the offer of the breakfast table. I was surprised when he ignored the over stuffed chair and sat on the wolf skin rug before the blazing fire. The staid and silent valet was as puzzled as I was when Dr. Weber took the poker and started raking out hot coals. Speaking one of his seven languages, he indicated to the valet he was to put the coffee pot on the coals, where it soon started perking. He again addressed his valet, leaving the poor man bewildered. Embarrassed that his master was acting with such lack of dignity, the valet awkwardly took a frying pan and bacon from the table and knelt down with difficulty beside his master. The two proceeded to cook their own breakfast. While attempting to make toast, the valet clumsily dropped two slices in the fire. Dr. Weber remonstrated "tut, tut" and took over the toasting fork with beaming delight. He was roughing it in the Northern wilds.

I tried not to look out the window to where Louis was sending frantic signals to hurry. Dr. Weber caught me signaling back not to interrupt as the toast was turning to cinders and the coffee boiling all over the hearth. Dr. Weber, smiling happily over the burnt bacon, said: "Tell Louis, no rush. Two weeks to get moose."

By the time Dr. Weber had changed into his hunting clothes, topped by a long tasseled stocking cap, Louis decided it was to late to go with the horses and they'd take the car instead. They headed for Dry Creek, about twenty-five miles from the ranch. Reaching Dry Creek, Louis saw moose tracks. He knew that, at that time of the year, the moose would be working their way up into the hills. Using binoculars, Louis spotted a moose in a burn about half way up. He knew its large rack of horns would please the doctor. My husband paid strict attention to the moose's location.

When Dr. Weber excitedly loaded Louis with cameras, film, lunch, jacket and high powered rifle, Louis decided he had so much to carry he better not take his own gun and said: "If you think your gun will do the job, I'll leave mine."

"Fine gun, shoot moose good" Dr. Weber emphatically assured him.

It was a long steep climb and Louis was careful to rest his hunter every few moments. They finally reached the burn. By the land mark of the big dry tree, Louis knew they were close. Cautiously moving along, they came out into a small opening. The burn was criss-crossed with fallen timber.

At any moment, Louis was expecting to see the moose feeding. Abruptly he stopped, thrusting out his arm he hissed a warning. A large silver-tipped grizzly was feeding in a small clearing about fifty yards from them. Now Louis noticed the immense palm of a moose horn sticking up. When the grizzly moved to the side, Louis was able to see the shape of a full grown moose with a light skiff of snow covering it. Either the bear had killed the moose or it had been shot by some hunter. Louis tried to point out the grizzly to Dr. Weber, whispering: "Doctor, Doctor, big grizzly."

Dr. Weber didn't seem to understand or even to hear. He kept saying "No, no. My moose. My moose."

There was a large dark stump about a hundred and fifty yards behind the grizzly, half hidden by young growth of willow and arctic spruce trees.

Dr. Weber raised his rifle. Instantly Louis knew by the barrel's elevation that that Dr. Weber was not aiming at the bear. It was now evident his hunter had mistaken the stump for a moose. The report and concussion of the heavy rifle, firing over the bear's head, caused the grizzly to clasp his paws over his head in a frenzy, rocking from side to side. Knowing at any moment the bear might charge, Louis hissed "Give me the gun."

Just then, the grizzly reared upright and for the first time Dr. Weber saw him. Shocked that the animal he wanted most to avoid was so close to him, he started yelling in panic: "BEAR! BEAR! BEAR!"

The grizzly roared as it paced back and forth, not wanting to leave the moose. Louis didn't want to jerk Dr. Weber's rifle out of his hands, but he knew the grizzly was trying to make up its mind whether or not to charge by the way it kept feinting jumps towards them.

Suddenly Dr. Weber came out of his paralysis and thrust his gun at Louis. "No grizzly, No grizzly."

Once more, the bear circled the moose, growling menacingly. "How many shells in gun?" Louis hissed, not knowing how many might be left after the one shot had been fired.

Dr. Weber jammed a hand into his pocket, fumbled about and brought out five shells, indicating to Louis to load the gun. Appalled that he had to put more shells in the gun because, from experience, he knew the slightest click of metal could bring on a charge, he hesitated. Then, seeing a bushy, dry arctic spruce beside them, he slowly reached in his pocket for a match. Striking it, he thrust the flaming match into the thick mat of branches. Blazing up, the whole tree became a flaming torch and under the cover of the crackling fire, Louis hurriedly loaded the rifle and fired twice over the grizzly's head.

Growling, the bear began to back up. Another shot, closer to his head this time, and he turned and stalked up the mountain. Louis grinned: "Well we bluffed that old codger, now we can go after the moose."

Dr. Weber had, had enough "No! No! Home Louis, We lucky we are alive."

That evening the valet and I listened with amazement as Dr. Weber pacing around and around the fireplace, flailing his arms, the tassel on his cap jerking spastically, related their harrowing experience. Louis crouched beside the blazing logs, almost convulsed with merriment wondering what the Doctor would have done had the grizzly charged. Exhausted by his close call, he excused himself to retire with his valet hovering solicitously over him. Turning as he left, our tired guest shook his head: "Oh, I lucky to be alive!"

Through the years, guests have come and gone but the Yukon has always given them an experience they will never forget. True to her mystery and her magic, the Yukon constantly gives each guest something they will always remember.

Chapter 5

GREAT FOR GRAYLING

We were standing on the wharf at Mayo, on the Stewart River in the Yukon, when my husband, Louis, looked at me with concern and said:"I guess I'm crazy to let you go with the pack train without me."

"But Louis," I pleaded, "you've made it easy for me. I'll only have our chief guide, Lonny Johnny, and our wrangler, Gordon Mervyn, to cook for and the horses are only carrying their rigging."

My husband hesitated. "What if it rains? You'll have muskeg trails for three days and you know it can be hell if it rains."

"Well it hasn't rained for weeks and look." We stared overhead. The sun looked as if it had been clipped from a Florida ad and pasted on our Yukon sky.

Still Louis was uneasy. "I shouldn't have taken this other guiding job just before our big game hunt," he said.

"Oh, yes you should. You might guide that geologist to a gold mine and besides..."

"Why are you so dead set on going anyway?" Louis gave me a sharp glance. "I'll be flying out with the rest of the guides and supplies in six days and you can wait for me here in town."

The roar of the float plane drowned out my voice. Pat Callison, our bush pilot, was getting ready for take off. He was flying Louis and Guy McMasters, a geologist from New York, to Crystal Lake. To make himself heard above the roar, Louis shouted in my ear. "Remember, you've got just six days to make it to Brown's lake before the hunters get there." I nodded in agreement.

"And another thing. Don't loose any horses. We need all of them."

I nodded with understanding.

"And take care of your men. See they have plenty of warm clothes."

I nodded with concern.

Pat yelled, "OK Louie, let's go."

Louis hurriedly pecked me on the cheek. "Don't forget, you have just six days, and that doesn't allow for any mishaps."

He strode across the wharf. I couldn't help grinning to myself. He hadn't even suspected. Four days would get us to Beaver River, where grayling fishing at this time of year was out of this world.

Louis grabbed his duffle bag, and yelled over his shoulder: "Get out of Keno before night or the horses will turn back home, your men will get drunk and God only knows what else could happen."

I smiled to myself as I watched him climb into the plane. I had really fooled him this time. Now, I'd have a chance at the best fishing...

The closed plane door flew open. "And don't fish. You won't have time."

The plane taxied down the Stewart River and I kicked an empty gas can. How on earth had my husband guessed? Well, I'd make time. I'd run the tails off those horses because after the arrival of our hunters I wouldn't have time to cast a fly.

I climbed into our truck and headed for Keno City, 45 miles north. It was at the end of the road and the start of the trail, leading to our hunting area in the Ogilvie Mountains.

Trouble was waiting me in Keno City. Tootsie, one of our best pack horses had been kicked by one of the other horses. Her hock was swelling fast and she could hardly walk. Gordon, looking longingly at the nearby Silver Queen hotel beer parlor, spoke as if the Gods had just created an opportunity for a very thirsty wrangler. "We'll have to stay here tonight," he smirked, and started taking off Tootsie's rigging.

"OH NO, we won't," I snapped, remembering my husband's warning.

"Then shoot her," Gordon barked, keen with disappointment. " You ain't go'n to get me to drag her all the way to Brown's Lake."

"You won't have too. Give me your lariat rope." I tied Gordon's lariat onto Tootsie's halter rope and signaled Lonny Johnny to get started. Lonny Johnny led us past the hotel and I dragged Tootsie past the amused miners shouting "Good luck. Bag plenty of trophy horns. See you next fall." An hour out of Keno City, and Gordon galloped back, "Cripes, can't you keep up?"

"How can I with Tootsie?"

"Hell, at the rate you're travelling, it'll be Christmas before we get to Brown's Lake."

"Have you any suggestions?"

29

"Shoot her."

"Don't forget, we need every horse and if I can keep her going today, her joint won't stiffen and she may be a lot better tomorrow."

We should have made it to Maynord Creek by the first night, but we were only half way. A grizzly had made a mess of the cabin at the wood camp and we had to sleep outside. In the middle of the night I awoke with rain pelting my face. Disgusted, I pulled the tarp over my head and never woke again until I heard Gordon grumbling to Lonny, "My boots are sop'n wet."

The men pulled an old stove out of the cabin and while I was coaxing the fire, Gordon padded around bare footed, saddling the horses, while Lonny Johnny went to look for a couple of strays.

Remembering Louis's instructions to look after the men, I balanced Gordon's soggy boots on two sticks of green wood atop the stove, then decided I'd run down to the little lake and make a couple of quick casts, while the fire was gathering momentum and the water was getting hot.

On the second cast a fish jerked my line. It was small but maybe the next would be larger. One after another I landed 10 small grayling. Beaver River was where I'd really get the big ones. Just one more cast then I'd have to get breakfast.

An explosive yell from Gordon made me jump. Dashing up the bank I saw my wrangler standing over the stove, holding up a pair of smoking boots. "OH GORDON!!! this is awful. What will you do now?" I wailed, watching one sole curl up and drop to the ground.

Gordon was too stricken to answer.

Thinking of the brushy trails ahead, I felt a growing panic at the thought of Gordon riding through it with bare feet in the stirrups. He would arrive at Brown's lake with bloody stumps and what would Louis say?

Desperately searching through the old cabin I found a pair of old rubbers the grizzly had tested his teeth on, leaving extra and unnecessary ventilation. Gordon was a good sport, declaring: "Sure I can make it to Brown's Lake in them, then your old man can send in and get me a new pair of boots."

Lonny returned with the strays and I was buckling on my .22 colt handgun when, for about the hundredth time, Lonny Johnny said:"Gee, that good gun. Fine gun that one. Bet'm shoot'm good."

I unbuckled the belt. "Here wear it."

Lonny grinned happily. "OK, we go now."

We set off in a drizzle spiked with sleet. The moss sopped up the rain like a sponge and then the trails began to float. Tootsie, lamer than on the previous day, dragged back, pulling the rope tight across my leg until I wanted to scream. My arms ached from hauling her up to ease the rope on my leg. Through the downpour I could see Lonny's white shirt gleaming. I wondered how an Indian could possibly be so tough as to ride through this deluge in his shirt sleeves.

Ahead I heard Gordon shout, "WHOA, WHOA damn you!" Bunny, the horse carrying our grub and sleeping bags, was mired in the mud. Lonny Johnny galloped back to help. We swung from our horses, sinking to our knees in ooze. I was surprised to see Lonny's teeth chattering, "For goodness sakes Lonny, put on your jacket or you'll catch pneumonia," I said.

"No jacket me."

"WHAT!!"

Lonny grinned sheepishly. "Forget'm"

"Do you realize this is an 80 day hunt. Snow before we get back and....well here." Remembering Louis's concern that his men have warm clothes I tossed the chief guide my down jacket.

Gordon, Lonny and I pushed and pulled until Bunny came out of the mud like a cork out of a bottle.

We climbed to a bench and were making good time when I heard the staccato crack of the .22. Tootsie wrapped me and my horse, Shorty, around a gnarled spruce tree and the pack string stampeded in all directions.

I was furious with myself for having loaned Lonny my gun. When I saw Lonny Johnny beaming from ear to ear holding up a blue grouse I choked down my words of wrath.

I was to regret it later. In the afternoon I kept hearing the Sing..g..g..g. of the .22 and Gordon and I were slowly going crazy trying to keep the horses on the trail.

That night at Eight Mile cabin Bunny wasn't among the pack horses waiting to be unsaddled. "Gordon, I would have thought you would have kept track of Bunny since she's carrying our beans and beds."

"With Lonny blasting ahead and you dragging behind, how in hell do you expect a wrangler to keep this pack string together?" Gordon stormed.

Gordon and Lonny went back to look for Bunny and about midnight we glumly ate cold beans.

Next night we reached McKay Hill in a downpour. The old cabin looked as if it was under a waterfall.

I knew if I was ever going to get to Beaver River in time to fish I was going to have to get back my gun.

Next morning I was up early, strapping on my gun. Lonny watched me out of the corner of his eye. Just before we mounted he nonchalantly announced: "Today we go up McKay Hill pass."

I stared at him in astonishment and disbelief. Lonny knew good and well I wanted to fish Beaver River. His black, beady eyes watched me through half slits. Although I had the advantage of a higher education, I knew Lonny Johnny, who could neither read or write, had outsmarted me. McKay Hill bypassed Beaver River.

I flung off the gun belt and threw it at him, gritting my teeth. "Lonny Johnny, from now I'll put pepper, the black stuff you hate, on everything you eat."

Lonny, buckling on the .22 colt, merrily chuckled. With a triumphant grin he said: "OK, now we go Beaver River way."

It stopped raining and Tootsie was walking with only a slight limp. Without a pack it was easy for her to keep up. My spirit began to soar. About noon we should be at my fishing hole. Before we reached the Beaver, it began to drizzle again and my grayling haven didn't look as glamorous as I remembered.

Instead of stopping to make tea and catch a few fish to pan fry for lunch, the men rode right past, eating lunch in their saddles. I was furious, swinging from my saddle yelling, "I'M GOING TO FISH!"

I tied Shorty to a spruce tree and yanked out my fishing gear. Since I was good enough to let Lonny have my gun, he could have stopped for an hour.

The Beaver River is fed by small streams issuing from the Ogilvie Range, part of the backbone of the great Rocky Mountain system. The Beaver, where it joins the Stewart is swift, but here it meandered, slow and sluggish, an ideal place for grayling.

Five casts and no luck, so I moved down the river. With the next cast my line wrapped around a willow and the fly kerplunked into the dark water. A grayling cleared the surface and grabbed the fly on it's downward dive. That's why I like grayling. They bite just as well for an amateur as for an expert. The grayling bored into deeper water, then abruptly ceased struggling and I worked him to shore. I took a step closer to lift him but my foot never came down. Instead my head swivelled in all directions. Directly under my raised foot was the largest,

32

freshest grizzly track I had ever seen. When I saw dung still steaming 10 feet from me I threw pole, fly and fish into the river and plowed through the brush in search of Shorty and my gun.

Shorty and I scuttled down an old caribou trail after the packtrain. I was looking over my shoulder when Shorty plowed to such a sudden stop I almost went over his head. He had stopped at the edge of a massive mud slide. As far as I could see the old trail had been obliterated by boulders, uprooted trees and mud. Below was an impassable canyon. Shorty turned and went straight up the mountain following the imprint of shod hooves in the caribou moss. I listened hopefully for the crack of the .22 which would slow down the outfit, but there was only a cry of a raven.

We lunged up staggering slopes, only to slide down from dizzying heights. Brush dragged my legs back until I wanted to scream. Branches of dwarf arctic spruce snapped back, blinding me. A cow moose and her calf, half submerged in a pot hole, crashed off into the timber. Fresh grizzly signs were all along the trail. Shorty, ploughing through a patch of muskeg, gave a sudden lunge, tossing me out of the saddle. I jumped up, clawing muck out of my eyes and ran after my departing horse. Panting with a severe pain in my side, I caught up with Shorty where he had anchored himself with one hoof on the reins.

Why in blazes didn't Lonny fire that blasted .22? He wanted it badly enough. In the pass leading down to Brain Creek, I stopped Shorty to glass ahead. With relief I caught a glimpse of a horse. I could see another mud slide ahead, so I kept Shorty up on the ridge until we cleared. Finally dropping down to Brain Creek, we travelled for hours between five and six foot high walls of blue glacier ice.

I was bitter with disappointment. Brain Creek looked much to small for any worthwhile fishing. I was still furious with Lonny. I was also half starved. Most of our grub had been lost when Bunny mired.

At last through the trees I saw a campfire flickering. The men had unpacked and were drinking tea while caribou ribs were roasting. They had shot the bull just before pulling into camp. I glared at Lonny. "Why didn't you wait so I could fish and I might have been lost?"

Lonny looked at me with amazement. "Why worry me? You got gun, lots of matches, lots of shells"

Since I held a chief guide's license I didn't dare tell them how scared I had been or they would think it a big joke for a guide to fear a few bear tracks. But I knew if I ran into a grizzly, the first thing

Shorty would do would be lighten his load. Years of secretarial work at a desk hadn't conditioned me to ride a pitching horse.

Lonny waved his hand towards the creek. "Lots of water"

"For minnows" I snapped and stomped off to set up my tent beside the fishless stream.

The next morning Gordon woke me with a yell: "Cripes, look at all the fish. WOWEEEEE!"

Lonny hollered: "Lots of fish. Lots of grub."

Gordon gave another yell, "Dolores, roll out and see WOW!"

They were just teasing. Making fun of my love for fishing. Well, I wouldn't give them the satisfaction of making a fool out of me and I rolled over and covered my head. But the men pushed my tent over and I had to crawl out. The sun was shining brightly. I couldn't believe my eyes, After all the heavy rains the creek was so clear one could see the rocks on the bottom. Here the creek made a wide bend and the water was so still you could hardly see it move and as far as you could see were grayling. The bright sun seemed to spotlight the fish, making them look like water nymphs in shimmering, iridescent shades of greens and blues. A breathtaking scene.

While I stood stunned with overwhelming joy, Gordon whacked off a willow for a pole and taking line and hooks from his pocket shoved it into my hand. "Here, your so nuts on fishing."

I watched dozens of big grayling surface for my fly. When the tug came I didn't have enough strength to pull it out. I just wanted the beauty and wonder of the moment to last forever.

Lonny grinned happily at me. "We good friends now?"

"Yes, Oh yes Lonny, Your the best guide in the whole Yukon."

Gordon was growing impatient. "Well, cripes,, I'm hungry. With all this fish I ain't go'n to eat mush for breakfast. If you ain't goin' to catch any, give me that pole"

I jerked the pole out of Gordon's reach. "Get yourself another one."

Gordon made another lunge for my pole and I slipped, sitting down in glacier cold water to my arm pits. After the first shock I noticed the water boiling around me with fish and a big fellow swarm across my lap.

Remembering a scientific report about the different species of fish, I held a 12 inch dorsal finned grayling under Lonny's nose. " What does this fish smell like?"

Lonny snorted, "you go crazy?"

34

"No, really Lonny, some scientists say grayling smells like thyme. Other scientists say they smell like cucumber. What do you think?"

Lonny gave me a puzzled look. "What's thyme? What's cucumber?"

As fast as Gordon and I caught fish, Lonny gutted them and tossed them into the frying pan. Gordon and I kept yelling to each other, claiming the largest fish.

"PLANE! PLANE COMI'N!!" Lonny yelled, dropping the frying pan.

A plane flying low, coming up the Brain, dipped it's wings and dropped a salt box, missing me by inches. I tore off the lid and read aloud "Honey, finished early. Hunters will be four days late, so go back to Beaver River. Will meet you there and you can do some grayling fishing. Your loving husband, Louis."

Lonny, Gordon and I helplessly looked at each other, then turned to gaze after the departing plane gliding so effortlessly over that tortuous back trail of mud slides and muskeg to Beaver River.

Lonny grabbed a grayling and contemptuously slid it under his nose, then savagely flung it into the creek. "Damn grayling stink like fish."

Chapter 6

GOD AND GRIZZLIES

Had I known before leaving the Olympia, Washington that I'd have seventeen close encounters with grizzlies, the Yukon would never have seen me.

I went to the Northern wilderness believing my faith in God was as unshakable as the rock of Gibraltar and as steadfast as the Statue of Liberty. The first grizzly I barged into shrivelled my faith to that of Minnie Mouse.

It happened when our big game hunting party camped on Wind River, in central Yukon. I was running down the trail to see a caribou killed by wolves the night before and now anchored by it's horns in a shallow riffle of the river. I rounded a thick grove of willows and skidded to an abrupt stop. Facing me was a full grown grizzly. With no gun and no tree to climb, I stood petrified, twenty feet from one of the most feared wild animals on the continent. The grizzly reared up on his hind legs to his full awesome and terrifying height to look me over. I called on God as he had never been pleaded with before, but it seemed God had left the Yukon. My heart began shooting blood through my veins as if I were taking off for outer space. Every muscle was alerted for fast action. The grizzly cocked his head from side to side, to get a better look at the pale, shivering creature in front of him. The wind started blowing his long silvery hair in waves over his huge body and it flashed through my mind that he was beautiful. He started rocking, making him come even closer. I sent up a more urgent call for help. This time there was an answer. The grizzly dropped back down and meandered off into the brush. Later I was to learn not all grizzlies are so obliging.

Because my husband expected me to expire at the sight of a grizzly, I shunned the humiliating truth and rearranged the incident in the telling. "My nerves were as calm as a hot summer day."

Louis snorted. "Your nerves won't be so damn calm if you ever meet a grizzly's full charge."

"That I can do without," I laughed uneasily, "besides, I don't have a gun."

"I'm giving you my Winchester 270. I've shortened the stock and softened the recoil with a rubber pad. You better start practicing."

"No thanks, it kicks."

"Kick or not, your life may depend on being able to shoot."

His words were prophetic, as proved when the hunting party was camped on Carpenter Creek and I had to meet a grizzly's full charge. The full account of this harrowing experience is told in my book White Squaw. Because I hadn't been sure where to place my shots and only luck had made the one shot fatal, I practiced to become another Annie Oakley, or Little Sure Shot, as Sitting Bull, called her. The training paid off when a grizzly put me up a cache.

Cache's are to me what bee hives are to bees — security. I knew I was in trouble when I went to cut some steaks and found several quarters of moose and caribou missing from the meat rack and grizzly hair stuck on the pole. Knowing he'd be back, I hurriedly carried all the trophy heads to the cache and hauled them on top. Minutes before he returned to clean up camp, I climbed on top of the cache. How he spent the whole night in trying to knock me off the cache is given a full account in my book Yukon Trophy Trails.

A grizzly had me up a cache another time but, luckily, he wasn't interested in staying. The trick is being able to differentiate between a grizzly's curiosity and his hostility in time to not take the wrong action. In other words, not to kill him if he's only scaring hell out of you. Sometimes it takes nerves of iron. When I read about a man who must have had nerves of granite, I told my husband, "Grizzly Adams used grizzlies to pack supplies to miners in California. It'd be fun to have a grizzly for a pet."

Louis hooted· "You and Adams are both crazy."

Over at Carpenter Lake I had a pet grizzly. Almost. We were on our way to see a large caribou migration when we came upon this skin ny young grizzly. There were no wild berries that year and he was starving to death. He looked so pathetic and cute. Now was my chance to have a pet. I fished for him, fed him table scraps and all the meat trimmings. When I was trying to find a name for him, Louis, snorted "Call him Dynamite, he'll be exploding into camp soon"

When Dynamite tangled in the tent ropes and knocked a pot of beans off the campfire in order to help himself, I knew he was getting tame.

It was a little disconcerting. Under my tender care Dynamite was filling out his hide and becoming a big grizzly. It was sometimes startling to bump into him at unexpected places. Our big game hunters didn't share my enthusiasm for my camp mascot and when Dynamite tried to move in with them, there were such strong objections it became obvious, we either had clients or we had Dynamite. The matter was settled one night when Dynamite decided to inspect the cook tent. The wrangler lost his cool and took a shot at him. I heard Dynamite groan and I was furious. The returning hunters reported seeing Dynamite streaking it over the pass heading for a kill they had just made.

The first year I acquired my big game Outfitters license, I also acquired my first grey hair. We were camped on the Snake River, not far from the border of the Northwest Territories. I was busy in the cook tent when I heard an ungodly noise. Grabbing my rifle I dashed out to face three grizzlies roaring with such volume it seemed to shake the ground under my feet. They were vocalizing an order to get off their game trail. To move a large hunting camp with such short notice was impossible. They weren't going to detour and started crossing a small side stream between us. I placed a shot in front of them. The wrangler, hearing the shooting, came running and we put several shots under and over them. They roared louder, determined to continue their journey through the middle of camp. We built a large camp fire on the trail and I sat up all night with the rifle across my knees. I had a lot of time to do some serious thinking. I came to the conclusion, maybe I'd live longer if I wasn't an outfitter. I finally set some brush on fire and they detoured, still grumbling their annoyance with squatters.

I never thought a grizzly could ever make me laugh, but one old fellow did when the pack train was working down through a pass to Snake River. Mountains rose steeply on either side of the trail so the horses were in a tight line. It was fall and the red soap berries grew thick along the trail. Suddenly the horses exploded in all directions, scattering up the steep mountain side, some rolling back down. I didn't want to take the chance of Shorty capsizing on top of me so I spurred him straight ahead. We rounded a large boulder and Shorty reared with a scream. In the middle of the trail a grizzly was flat on his back, raking soap berries onto his chest, then with the other paw scooping the berries into his mouth. The commotion of the terrified pack train never fazed him. He was having a sumptuous feast and nothing under Northern skies was going to interrupt. We detoured.

Snake River was so heavily populated with grizzly it was impossible for me to have a good night's sleep. Every little sound woke me and with good reason, our camps were continually being raided. Towards the end of the hunt I was so dead tired from lack of sleep, my husband radioed our bush pilot and I flew back to Mayo.

It was a twenty mile drive to the home ranch. The fall colouring was gorgeous. The tape deck played Rachmaninoff's Rhapsody, the perfect background music while enjoying such beautiful scenery. I sank back into the seat relaxing and thinking it was such a relief to be free of bears. Rounding a curve I trounced hard on the brake. Standing upright at the side of the highway were three grizzlies. As if they were hitchhikers successful in stopping a car, they ambled towards me. I stepped on the gas, realizing that in the Yukon, you're always in grizzly country.

Our log cabin home overlooks a lake which often reflects Hungry Mountain where, now and then, caribou can be seen. In spring and fall large Vs of sand hill cranes and Canadian honkers clamorously call 'hello' as they return with the sun or 'good-bye' as they shrilly vocalize their departure. The dazzling white of the swans against a deep fathomless blue sky brings magic to the wilderness. Bears and moose are in the valley.

Three large picture windows overlook this panorama. I am always glancing out to check on the activities of wild life. One day I glanced out just as a grizzly plunged into the lake from the opposite shore. His head bobbing across looked massive. Looking through the binoculars his tracks in the sand looked huge. Curious to find out how large, I grabbed the tape measure, ran down the trail and shoved my canoe into the water. Ten pounds of love and spunk jumped in wagging his tail. We watched the grizzly splash out, climb the bank and disappear into the brush. Now was my chance. Feeling safe I shored in a gooey mess of mud and climbed out, ordering Punky to stay in the canoe. The bear tracks were further away than I had calculated, but I kept plowing through the mud. I had to pull hard each step I took to get my foot free. The measurements exceeded the size of any bear tracks I had ever seen. Ten and a half inches wide and fifteen inches long.

Punky brought me out of my amazement with sharp staccato bark. I looked up to see a geyser of water spout up as a grizzly plunged into the lake, heading for our side. Calculations flashed through my mind. Could the bear swim faster than I could plow back through the mud? I was half way to the canoe when the grizzly was three quarters of the way across. I picked up speed. Punky was barking his head off. The grizzly splashed to shore. Acting puzzled over Punky's yipping, he hesitated, giving me time to tumble into the canoe and paddle enough distance to give me a good head start in case he tried to follow. Instead, he stretched out on the sand and seemed to forget I existed.

In grizzly country, a dog can either save you or get you into trouble. Louis and I were picking wild black currants and since we would be together, only Louis took his gun. To sound the alarm in case a bear was in the berry patch, I took one of our huskies. Taku went about his own business, for which I could have killed him later. I found a new patch of berries some distance from Louis. My pail was half full when a blur of bodies flashed past, upsetting my pail and sending berries in all direction. Taku was in hot pursuit of a grizzly, chasing him up the hill. I screamed for him to come back, an order he promptly obeyed by getting in front of the grizzly and chasing him back down. They passed about fifty feet in front of me. The grizzly was a beautiful color, a rich shade of ivory with chocolate brown legs. He was very young or Taku would never have gotten away with it.

I yelled "GRIZZLY" expecting Louis to come running with the gun. To my astonishment he kept walking in the opposite direction. As I was speeding towards him, Taku chased the grizzly between us. When I caught up with my husband I was at the boiling point. " Why didn't you come with the gun? A grizzly almost ran over me!"

Louis looked at me with astonishment. "I thought you were yelling `Lize' and I wondered why in hell you were yelling `Lize'."

That wasn't the only time Taku got me tangled with a grizzly. Once I was driving to town with Taku sitting beside me. From the heavy growth of brush at the side of the highway a grizzly dashed out in front of the car. I slammed on the brake, but he didn't like the nudge the bumper gave him and he gave the car hood a permanent dent. Taku took exception and lunged across me to the open car window. With my arms and lap full of husky, I was immobilized for a moment. This grizzly was mad and being twice as large as the husky, Taku wouldn't have a chance, although by his snarls he thought he could chew the grizzly to pieces. As Taku sailed through the window, I grabbed his tail with both hands and hung on until the grizzly gave the husky's head a knock out swat and I had to let go. Taku leaped for the bear's throat but the grizzly was to fast. Seeing this was going to develop into a battle with no holds barred, I rammed the grizzly. As he rolled into the ditch, I yanked Taku into the car and took off with my wheels spinning.

When I purchased my small English Anglia, I wasn't thinking

about grizzlies. Had I been, I would have purchased a semi-trailer. I was driving my little car to town when I had a flat tire. I had never changed a flat tire, that being in my husband's department, and I had no idea how to do it, but I did know the car had to be jacked up and the nuts taken off the wheel. I was accomplishing this with some difficulty when I had a feeling something was behind me. There had been no sound, just an uneasiness. I looked up into the car window and froze. Reflected, were the images of three grizzlies across the highway. A mother and her two year-old cubs, almost as large as she was. I knew if I made any quick move it might trigger her protective instincts so I was afraid to dive for the car door. If I tried crawling under the car, my wiggling legs might bring out their hunting instinct. They were use to grabbing flopping salmon. In slow motion, inch by inch, I crept around behind the car, then made a leap for the car door, just as one of the cubs started rearranging the tools. I jolted off the jack and drove as no other flat tire has ever been driven, all the rest of the way to town. Louis was shocked when he had to pay for a whole new wheel.

When first I saw my husband's registered Scotch Highland cattle, I thought their colouring was the same as some of the grizzlies I had seen. Several times they had rammed my heart into my throat when I had come upon one of the herd unexpectedly.

After a week in bed with the flu, I felt badly in need of exercise and went in search of my saddle horse. I felt pretty weak and my Winchester 270 felt heavy but I plodded along the trail, with the hope Shorty hadn't strayed too far. Suddenly I was startled when willows about fifty feet in front of me thrashed around and a patch of tawny fur showed through a small opening. Against all my training from our Indian guides and my husband, I fired. Waiting a few moments to gain courage, I parted the brush and looked down in horror. At that moment I would gladly have faced ten grizzly charges rather then have to tell my husband I had shot one of his precious cows.

I have a certain empathy with grizzlies. We have the same prob lem. Civilization is moving in on us. To meet the requirements of our type of existence means retreating further back into the wilderness. The question is, will we have to retreat onto the endangered species list and on into extinction? If this happens, the world will loose one of the most noble of animals and people like me, a Northern frontier pioneer, will be but a memory.

Chapter 7

PETS OR PILLS

Billy DeChuck, our old Indian neighbor, fearfully looked at me and started backing toward the door. Puzzled, maybe he hadn't understood, he snapped "What that you say?"

"I said I was going crazy."

In a quandary, Bill hesitated. "Why for you say that?"

"Because I'm so lonesome I could die."

Old Billy's weathered, wrinkled face broke into a relieved grin. "You no go crazy."

"Oh, yes I will." How could I explain to this primitive mind? Ever since my husband had left to guide a geologist for a large mining company into the Bonnet Plume area, I had been attacked by an enemy I never knew existed. This terrifying loneliness was destroying any semblance of rationality. It was a dark fog of despair and desperation sweeping over me, blotting out all I had cherished. Supporting my fears were the many Northern tales of people succumbing to the long winter's solitude by various degrees of derangement.

Billy, regaining his courage, sat down again and, after consuming all my bread and strawberry jam and drinking a quart of tea, seemed suddenly inspired. "You knows longs times ago, lot's guys climb big hill."

"Oh, you mean the Chilkoot Pass, during the Klondike gold rush?"

"Yea, yea, that what I mean, they pack lot's stuff."

"Yes, I know, pianos, stoves, Parisian gowns and ..."

"Cats" Billy blurted.

"CATS? Why on earth would they pack cats over that brutal trail?"

"Sell to guys lonesome. You get cat, no go crazy."

"But I want people," I wailed.

"AH hh," Billy snorted in disgust. "Lots people look alright, talk alright, no good inside. Cat, he good, all time. You get cat."

After Billy threatened to stop chopping wood if I didn't get a cat, I headed for town with no intention of getting a cat. Hopefully, no one would even think of parting with a cat and even if they did, I'd concoct some excuse to appease Billy.

I was sure Billy was mixed up about cats. Just like he had been when he told of white man killing off all the Indians at the old trading post of Lancing with wolf poisoning. In fact, it had been the flu.

But in the back of my mind were the nagging remembrances of having stood in old rotting cabins of long gone prospectors and trappers, miles from any other habitation, and seeing cat walks circling the ceiling to keep some feline pet off of drafty floors and platforms built under stove pipe elbows to keep tabby warm. I had often wondered why they kept cats way out in the bush.

Weeks later, I read Pierre Berton's book, Klondike, and found they actually did pack cats over the Chilkoot pass and sold them to lonesome prospectors for an ounce of gold apiece. In town I stopped to visit Mrs. Don Baker. At the moment, she was cuddling five wide eyed kittens. She greeted me with "you wouldn't want a kitten?"

I quickly hedged:"Our huskies would gobble them up in one gulp."

Mrs. Baker snapped back "train your dogs to leave the kittens alone." She thoughtfully shook her head. "I simply can't keep all five. I'll have to give three away."

It wasn't the three little anxious faces with black and white markings that made me swallow a definite, NO. It was old Billy's stern face that flashed in my mind. If he really did stop chopping wood, I'd freeze because I never seemed to get the hang of swinging an axe.

Deciding it would be easier to endure a cat than the cold, I said: "Oh, alright, I'll take one, but which one?"

"Take all three," Mrs. Baker replied without hesitation.

So three tiny fluffs of bewilderment were stuffed in a cardboard box and deposited in the car seat beside me. Barely an icy mile had slipped under the tires when there was a frustrated mewing, followed by frantic scrambling, then one small face pecked out. Deciding he wasn't afraid of this big world, a ball of fluff tumbled over the side of the box. Knowing the danger of slamming on brakes while driving on icy roads, I let the little explorer alone. There was a mad scampering up my fur parka, a soft purring buzzed under my right ear, more clawing up my parka hood, then the kitten curled up in the wolf ruff on top of my head and went to sleep. Just before reaching the ranch I slowed to go down a steep, slippery grade. Half way down the car started to spin dizzily. There was a mad scrambling on top of my head and tiny claws dug in until I felt pin pricks, but he stuck on, convincing me he

43

was surely a descendent of one of the kittens who made it over the treacherous Chilkoot pass. What would be a fitting name for this fluff of tenacity? I remembered hearing about a man named Tom who hiked over the Pass fifty-six times. There and then my over head passenger received his name Chilkoot Tom, only it turned into Tommy Boy, a more endearing appendage.

Driving into the yard I saw Billy, sitting where the wood pile should be, toying with the axe. Striding to the car, he looked like an Indian on the war path, but when Tommy Boy leaped from my head through the open window onto Billy's shoulder he became more like a clucking mother hen. The old Indian was delighted and later, when I looked out the cabin window, the wood pile was so high I couldn't believe my eyes.

The huskies always started their mournful laments when the shadows slunk into the darkness of night. They sounded as lonesome as wailing banshee's sending me in a frantic search for the bottle of aspirin to dull the lonely desperation. The kittens had been playing with the bottle and not being able to find it I flung myself on the sofa and howled with the huskies.

A screechy yowling joined the chorus. All three kittens were yelling their heads off. Suddenly I realized they were hungry. Getting up, I cooked some mush, pouring a can of milk over it. They soon had mush smeared from end to end. Chins dripped milk, one eye closed with gobs of sticky oatmeal. They looked so comical I burst into laughter. With tummies full they curled up on the wolf rug in front of the crackling fire in the massive rock fire place and went to sleep.

When they awoke, they were three bundles of curiosity. I couldn't keep up with their energy.

The cold ashes in the fireplace were perfect for a good roll. The white curtains were great for climbing. To them life was so jolly good that I felt a hard knot inside starting to thaw. By bedtime I was so exhausted I fell into deep slumber and that was the end of my insomnia.

Tommy Boy was the extrovert of the three, developing a character equal to ten Charlie Meadows. He learned fast that you have to be tough to be a cat in the Yukon. He needed no father to teach him how to hunt. He learned it by first stalking big game animals on our home movie screen. Our brand new white movie screen has a permanent dent where Tommy Boy nailed a Camp Robber, flying across the screen with a pancake. He gave me a puzzled look as if saying "Where is that bird I caught?"

Old Billy made regular check up visits and would tease: "You lonesome?" Then we both burst out laughing. It seemed miraculous to me that pets had taken the place of pills and an old Indian's sagaciousness had solved my problem.

One day I accidentally left the door open while I dashed for some stove wood. Our big husky broke the snap on his chain and I spotted him sneaking into the cabin. Hastening to avert carnage, for I expected little would remain of my pets but fur, I skidded to a stop inside the door and stared in amazement. That big mutt of a Siberian, who had whipped a couple of wolves and tangled with a grizzly, was having his face thoroughly washed by two kittens while the third was playfully batting at his big plumed tail. From then on Taku was their ferocious, snarling guardian angel.

Louis returned in mid-winter to start trapping. He had the custom of keeping his bait scents on the top shelf of the corner cupboard, behind the Spode tureen with its beautiful clump of ceramic fruit on the lid. I had been to town shopping and when I returned, was presented with a brown paper sack. Something in it rattled. "A gift for me?" I asked expectantly.

Louis grinned kind of sheepishly. "Well, yeah. From Tommy."

I opened the sack and shrieked "MY TUREEN". The lid was shattered into hundreds of little pieces.

Louis didn't seem to realize the calamity and, unbelievably in such a tragic moment, he was laughing.

"Tommy proved I've got the scents for my bait right. He climbed three shelves to get it. He was crazy over it and so was the lynx."

On a late winter day, Louis thought while there was still snow, he better haul some fence posts. As he was hitching the dogs to the toboggan, Tommy Boy was watching proceedings from the top of the woodpile. Suddenly he dashed in front of the team's leader and trotted ahead of the team up the trail. The temptation of that black feathery tail was to much for Zitzie to resist and he snapped at it, taking a few hairs and sending Tommy Boy into squeals of protest. All hell broke loose. Tommy's guardian angel took on the whole team, knocking Louis flat on his back onto the toboggan and battling it out on top of him. I'm sorry but I'll have to skip the next few moments. It's unprintable. But when Louis finally emerged from under the tangled mass, purple with rage, he grabbed the troublemaker by the tail and flung him into the cabin.

After the long, harsh, ice bound Yukon winter, spring is a miracle of new life. A contrast of vibrant ebullience of emotional appreciation. Fragrant earth, buoyant sun warmed air, chartreuse leafed trees, all celebrated by the return of mama bluebird announcing her arrival by singing her heart out on the top of a door side spruce tree, as she has for the past eight years.

Wide eyed with wonder, the kittens timidly sniff golden yellow daisies, curiously bat at lavender tinted butterflies and make themselves obnoxious nuisances to chattering squirrels.

With the snow gone and the golden sunshine thawing frozen ground, I placed the chaise lounge on the edge of the eighty-five foot bank overlooking the lake. Tommy Boy curled up on my lap. The pin tail grouse were drumming on their dancing grounds. Sand Hill cranes rose from far meadows, flying low over our heads. In a pond edging the lake, a mother mallard duck swam in search of a nesting place. This was the sixth year she had returned to raise a family.

Without warning a wide spread of grey wings swooped up the bank, darting down to fasten sharp talons into the back of the sleeping cat, The powerful wings vigorously flapped to get airborn. The sudden attack stunned me into inertia until Tommy Boy yowled. I threw the book I was reading with enough force to knock the Great Horned owl off balance and it dropped Tommy Boy, who streaked it to his guardian angel.

Later I heard of several owl attacks, including one on Glenn Naylor, a ranger in the Kananaskia Provincial Park. Although the Glenn was wearing a toque, the assault left him with a torn and bleeding scalp. It is believed the owl mistook his fuzzy toque for a rabbit. I was lucky our assailant didn't take my fuzzy hair for his lunch.

In the afternoon, Taku started barking in decibels, meaning, DANGER !!! HELP !!!HURRY!!!. We kept him on a wire run in front of the living room windows to warn of wolves, who often climbed the bank to visit the huskies. Running out, I was puzzled to see the husky in such a frenzy with nothing in sight but a whisky jack. Starting to return to the cabin, I heard a faint meow. I couldn't locate the sound but Taku kept insisting there was something in the thick branches of the spruce tree. Another faint meow and I saw a little black and white face peeking down from the trembling tip of the spruce tree. Below Tommy Boy was a bear. I quickly released the snap on Taku's collar and dragged him out of sight behind the cabin. The year-old black bear backed down the tree and a Commanche yell from me sent him scurrying down the bank and into the thick timber, but Tommy refused to come down even for a can of sardines.

When we are away on long hunting trips we leave our home in the care of Peter Ellis, a fine old Indian who doesn't share our devotion to Tommy. In fact, at the very sight of our pet, he goes into a rage, hurling such epitaphs as "you dumb tomcat" That's the trouble. Tommy isn't dumb. He outsmarts Peter. He finds ways of climbing over all of Peter's defenses and raiding the drying rack the Indian uses to smoke his winter supply of salmon. By the time we return, the skirmish over the tempting fish has escalated into a battle with Peter on the war path and Tommy Boy full of salmon.

Old Billy was making one of his visits when I started complaining. "Tommy is in mischief all the time. The other day, he dragged a baby duck up this high bank and now mother duck will never raise her family here again and Tommy wakes me every morning at the dreadful hour of six A.M."

"You lonesome"? Billy chortled, slyly glancing at me.

I stared blankly at the old Indian. I had forgotten I had ever been lonesome.

With Tommy Boy's next escapade, I was sure he was starting on his second round of nine lives. When the tractor was in need of repairs, Louis loaded it on our three-ton truck and I opened the gate for him to drive through. As he shifted into high gear, I had a fleeting glimpse of something black and white sitting on the tractor seat with white paws braced on the steering wheel. I ran screaming after the truck, but Tommy was too intently watching the road ahead to notice me. Louis was unaware he had a passenger until he parked in front of the Royal Canadian Mounted Police barracks and saw a familiar looking creature flash past and up the flag pole with a couple of town huskies hot on his tail. Louis gleefully reported what a picture Tommy made "with the red and white Canadian flag flapping over his head".

The trip was too much for Tommy and he contracted pneumonia. All I had on hand to meet the crisis was a bottle of Dr Bell's horse medicine. To cut the dosage down from that for a horse to that for a cat, I needed a computer. After mathematically filling a page with data I hoped Dr Einstein would approve of, I concocted a dose of three drops of Dr Bell to twenty-three drops of water. I hesitated to give the medication, painfully remembering I had flunked the first year of freshman algebra. What if I miscalculated and killed poor little Tommy? I shuddered.

I kept anxiously glancing at the cat who yesterday had been so joyfully riding the vacuum cleaner. Tommy's eyes were closed and he was as limp as flat beer. I gritted my teeth and poured a dose through his pried open teeth. No sign of life. In another fifteen minutes another dose, a flutter of an eye lid. Later another dose, a faint meow. Since he was shivering, I lay on the sofa, placed him on my chest and we both went to sleep. In the morning I was having trouble breathing. With every breath it felt as if I was lifting a ton. Fearing I had caught pneumonia from Tommy, I opened my eyes to find all three cats lying across my breast. Dumping them off, I was relieved when my breathing returned to normal. Tommy quickly recovered and was soon riding the vacuum cleaner again.

Sometimes an animal comes into your life with such an endearing personality it wraps it self right around your heart. People living isolated lives in the Far North realized the value of animals to relieve the ache of loneliness long before modern scientists acknowledged their merits.

More and more sophisticated health professionals have proven that a loving slurp from an affectionate dog or the nestling on the lap of a purring cat, can have enormous healing effect on sick or lonely people.

From this knowledge, a new treatment technique, known as Pet-facilitated therapy, uses animals to promote physical and mental health for troubled people. There is also a Pet Access League society (PETS) using the same approach.

According to Dr. Tom Ferguson, recent research has proven a pet can reduce blood pressure, alter the course of heart disease and decrease stress levels.

Dr. Leo Bustard, Dean of the college of Veterinary medicine at Washington State University, says: "I think the day is coming when doctors will sometimes prescribe pets instead of pills. For what pill could give you the love, laughter and endearment of a pet?"

I hope if you are suffering from any illness or just plain loneliness, that your physician will prescribe a pill like Tommy Boy.

Chapter 8

DON'T LET THE YUKON BLUFF YOU

At sometime in life, romance, adventure and greener pastures lurk in every woman's mind, and each year more women migrate to the Yukon — that dreamland of handsome, red-coated Royal Canadian Mounted Police singing The Indian Love Call. This invasion is not without its problems.

Born and raised in a highly technical society, the average American woman has no idea what it means to live in Canada's remote, non-technical frontier. So it isn't surprising that the locals believe American women are spoiled, which is perfect nonsense. It just takes a little longer for them to learn to live like prehistoric women wearing animal skins, and still longer to shift the taste buds from filet mignon, caviar and bouillabaisse to the delights of boiled caribou eyes and baked, ungutted fish. I was one of those naive American women when I left my fashionable apartment overlooking avenues of cherry trees in the fairy-tale splendor of Olympia, Washington, and moved to a log cabin amidst 207,000 square miles of permafrost in central Yukon Territory.

In the middle of this landscape, unchanged since the time of the mammoth, I wanted to create a home of elegant design, embodying comfort and beauty, even though the exterior of the cabin would retain an architectural style popularized during the Stone Age.

Luckily, I'm addicted to log cabins the way other people are to fine wines, opera or pizza. When my husband, a big game outfitter, built this rustic one-room original, he had no idea the inside was going to be professionally decorated. The windows were all sizes and canted at odd angles. The pole ceiling dripped caribou moss insulation, and the hand-sawed lumber floor — a triumphant accomplishment of muscle over gravity — had no boards of the same thickness.

When I wrote to my former schoolmates in Olympia with the news of my move, my acquired talents in interior design were about to be used to spruce up the inside of a trapper's cabin. The return-mail shock waves were of such intensity that I was glad I hadn't told them about signing up for a post-graduate course in northern wilderness living at Canada's "on-the-spot" university. If I flunked, I could freeze to death, be made into mincemeat by marauding grizzlies, evicted without notice by wolverines or made bloodless by mosquitoes.

Without any further encouragement from my former colleagues, I rolled up my sleeves and challenged the smoky, moose-grease splattered log walls with spontaneous combustion, only to find that underneath the grime the logs had been painted a dubious white.

My husband had warned that I'd be looking through windows at a landscape Old Man Winter kept in the deep freeze for seven months of the year. To have all that white, inside and out, for more than 200 days — impossible. I'd contract the worst case of cabin fever ever known. I needed contrast, something to bring that colourless monotony to bay.

Suddenly I remembered the French drapes I'd stuffed in the trunk at the last moment. Perfect! The vignette of color would foil winter's whiteouts. The billiard green background gave a warm, rich. vibrant glow to the jewel tones of the botanical bouquets printed on the cloth — luscious pink cabbage roses, periwinkle blue delphiniums, sun yellow irises and feathery silver sprays of statice. Let the temperature drop to 60, 70 or even 80 below. The cloth flowers would remind me that even the most fragile could survive.

New York's Mrs. Archibald Manning Brown, a leader in creating the famous American classic style of design, would surely think that matching the walls to the green background of the drapes would be the creme de la creme. My husband would simply have to paddle his canoe 20 miles to town and buy some billiard green paint.

Louis, my husband, disagreed. "I think yellow would be a better choice. Gets pretty dark here in the winter."

"Most certainly NOT! I'm sure Mrs. Archibald Manning Brown would insist it be billiard green."

Louis, still a little dazed over his success in convincing me that a trapper's cabin was just the place for developing my artistic talents, dutifully paddled to town for the paint. What he brought back was dark, bilious green stain, which should be used only on battleships.

"Make do with what you've got" became such a repeated refrain that I wondered why it was omitted from the national anthem. However, the stain obliterated the grime on the logs, so I figured it would effectively hide the worn spots on the linoleum as well. Remembering an old New England trick, I spattered several colours of paint on the newly green floor, hoping to match the drape's bouquets on the floor's basic green background, hoping the splotches would spread to form intriguing patterns.

Before starting to paint, we moved my husband's moose-horn, caribou-horn and twig furniture out onto the tundra, later to be partly replaced by my French collection then stored in a slab cache.

Louis, unnerved by the interruption of his previous lifestyle, took off for the mountains, leaving me happily splashing paint on the floor. Since I intended to paint myself onto the bed, I stacked it with sandwiches, cookies, tea and paperbacks. I'd have to stay abed until the paint dried, but, after all that expenditure of creative energy, I'd need the rest.

Later, I was reclining in bed, munching a caribou-meat sandwich and reading Veliskovsky's Worlds in Collision, all the while thinking how proper the set up. CRASH! BANG! CRASH! I bolted upright, certain Earth had smashed into something in outer space. CRASH! RIP! RIP! No, it sounded more like wood being dynamited.

I crawled to the foot of the bed. From there I could see through a small window to the nearest cache where we had stored our supply of dried moose meat. One look and I leaped into the middle of wet paint, grabbed my rifle and dashed out the door just as a grizzly wiggled his rear end through a newly constructed hole in the cache. Not wanting to shoot him in the fanny, I yelled, hoping to get him to reverse. No such luck. There wasn't even time to shoot. One moment he was there, the next he was inside amid the moose meat.

My parents had always tried to impress upon me that reason was man's basic means of survival. So, I reasoned that as long as the moose meat lasted the grizzly would be content and there was no need for me to risk my neck going in after him, or even to stay outside shivering. Therefore, I removed the small window to provide a clear field of fire, crawled back onto the bed and ate all the cookies to calm my nerves.

Meanwhile, Louis came back after some forgotten rifle shells and he reasoned that he wasn't going to let that grizzly eat all our moose meat. Later we used the old moocher's hide to cover the smears on the floor.

By the time the paint finally dried, it was 55 below. As we moved my furniture out of the slab cache, a big horned owl sat on the roof, hooting. The Indians say the owls are giving a message when they hoot, so I asked my husband what he thought the owl was saying.

Louis grinned. ''He doesn't fancy this French stuff. He's telling Louis XV to get the hell out of the Yukon.''

Once the elegant furniture was inside the cabin, I watched with horror as the etagere and kidney desk turned white with frost. I knew that if the antique, aged patina came off when it thawed my grandmother would leap out of her grave.

With more thawing, the finish on the diminutive bombe chest cracked. The summer before, when Louis transported my furniture across the Stewart River in a canoe, the chest fell overboard and it was sometime before we could fish it out. To salvage it back to respectability I used an ancient oriental art. The huskies had found an abandoned wild goose nest filled with frozen eggs. I glued crushed egg shells over the chest, applied glaze made of red ochre leached from a local deposit of iron ore, and rubbed it with oil from a freshly caught fish. Careful treatment of the raised areas left a beautiful porcelain-like finish. No cracks.

The Louis XV chairs met total disaster. In trying to find a comfortable way to sit in one, my Louis tilted and rocked back on the rear legs. The French chair lost the wrestling match and collapsed.

I sent an SOS to my friends, asking for instructions on how to mix my husband's bear, wolf and wolverine rugs with my needlepoint and hooked rugs; his Eskimo soap stone carvings with my Dresden and Lenox figurines; his diamond willow and horn furniture with my French antiques. I was trying to avoid the museum effect. The word came — character was back in the design vocabulary. If a stuffed wolverine snarling at a growling polar bear rug was character, our cabin would have it.

My four-poster, canopy bed created other difficulties. It gave my husband claustrophobia. "It's like sleeping under a brush pile," he grumbled. "Shuts off my breathing."

I couldn't help but remember a teasing remark made at our wedding. "It's like merging Madam Pompadour with Grizzly Adams."

That remark was recalled again later when I made a strenuous effort to recreate the specialties learned in classy French cooking schools. None of these exquisite foods impressed Louis. Instead, he got indigestion.

Not wanting to face widowhood with The Indian Love Call slowly freezing into crystallized echoes, I dutifully learned to cook a la aborigine. With nothing more complicated than moose stew, the kitchen shrank to a small corner. The only real problem was when meat was frying in the kitchen corner, the smoke descended like Los Angeles smog to the bedroom corner with devastating results. It was a hellish task getting the grease out of the filigree lace of the bed's canopy.

My design sources remained mute about how to handle our interior lighting problems without turning the cabin into a hardware store. Propane froze at 50 below, so there had to be kerosene lamps. Kerosene froze at 55 below so there had to be gas lanterns. If we ran out of gas, there had to be candles. If there were no more candles, there had to be special dishes for the moose grease lights, which gave off noxious billows of smoke and, if used for any length of time, would turn the white polar bear rug into a black bear rug.

Every American is partly raised in a bathroom. When Louis told me there would be no space in a one-room cabin for a bathroom, the last of The Indian Love Call faded into space. My husband laughed at my horror. "It was the outhouse that made the Vikings," he said.

He could laugh. These things are less complicated for men. At 70 below, it would take more than a plumber to thaw me out. After my first winter visit to the outhouse, I expected to be permanently frozen to the seat until spring.

Hanging the drapes was exasperating. The brackets couldn't be nailed to the chinking. Disgusted, I threw down the hammer. "This place is impossible."

"You told me in the States," Louis snorted, "that they renovate dilapidated old barns, school houses and chicken coops. You're not going to let a little old trapper's cabin lick you."

After that pep talk, effort was renewed, but I didn't know what effort was until that night. Glancing out the window to look at the moon, I looked into the gleaming yellow eyes of a wolf. The wolf pack, paying a social call on the huskies, was also interested in anything edible. Within minutes the drapes were hung and snapped shut.

Sometime later, feeling good about the cabin's face lift. I flopped into a chair and melted into my coffee. Without help from the occult, a crystal ball or Gloria Vanderbilt, I had amalgamated a crazy jigsaw puzzle. Grizzly Adams' wild, exuberant flamboyancy collaborated with Madam Pompadour's simple elegance, creating a beautiful blend of squaw-tanned moose hide and brocade upholstery, Meissen candlesticks and mammoth tusk carvings, filigree gold Baroque frames and grizzly paw lamps.

It was overwhelming to realize that I, Mrs. Louis J. Brown, had created for Canada the same uniqueness Mrs. Archibald Manning Brown had created for America. I had originated the Yukon classic style of design.

To celebrate, we drove the team of huskies to town for some of Yukon's over proofed rum. It wasn't proof against the dilemma we found back home. When a fire was started in the stove, smoke poured into the room.

"Something's plugging up the stove pipe," Louis growled, after considerable swearing.

Rushing onto the roof, he jerked up the stovepipe, scattering soot and ash throughout the cabin. A wolverine was frozen inside the pipe against the damper. Before we could start a fire, the carcass had to be thawed out of the pipe, a task that took most of a day.

A week later the sun sank behind Hungry Mountain and we began groping around in our green cave. Louis didn't help matters by saying, "Should have used yellow — reminds one of the sunshine that we won't see for two months."

The Yukon is noted for its extremes in weather, but in January it did the unthinkable — it rained. The dirt roof turned into a mud slide, which slid down through the pole ceiling and onto my freshly waxed floor. The only place not covered with mud was the bed. The canopy caught all the mud in the bedroom corner. Louis finally admitted that the canopy was good for something.

That February the temperature sank to 76 below and all rodents within commuting distance converged on our snug cabin. Mice found it easy to tunnel through the moss chinking, while squirrels preferred adding the demolished chinking to a messy conglomeration of shredded newspapers, egg cartons, oats, flour and glue to make their own snug little nests. The frost seeped in through the various excavations, turning the inside of the cabin into a refrigerator badly in need of defrosting.

With the first warm breezes of spring, I told Louis, "I'm so tired of green, I don't think I can stand to see the grass come up."

The warmer weather delighted the grouse. The roof first thawed around the stove pipe, giving the birds access to gravel. Scratching and pecking, the grouse generated a sandstorm below, covering everything with a fine grit.

"This is horrible," I wailed. "What can we do?"

"Build a new cabin," Louis said calmly. "You'll never be able to cover that green stain, even if you used a hundred coats of paint. And for God's sake, get your Yukon classic right the next time."

I'm working on it now. For a start, the fireplace will be of Klondike quartz, gleaming with gold nuggets stuck in the holes, and the color scheme will be all yellow.

The North has sneaky ways of weeding out the unsuspecting. It's only a matter of proving who's the toughest — you or the Yukon. And it comes with a million-year guarantee of white Christmases. With plenty of guts, one can call the Yukon's bluff and live happily ever after on a Christmas card.

Chapter 9

HOW TO TAME
A TRAPPER

I flew north in 1953 to marry a Yukon Territory trapper, envisioning closets full of muskrat, otter, and mink coats, a negligee trimmed with royal ermine, and our floors smothered in fur rugs. I had never heard of a fur auction.

Although school was behind me, my real education was just starting, with much of the knowledge I thought I had about to go down the drain. Some of the startling discoveries I was to make included the fact that animals make tracks, and that they have fleas, that wolves are not always meditating when they howl, and that the favorite pastime of nature's dear little creatures is gobbling each other up.

Our June honeymoon sped by, extending into a summer that came and went, and soon it was early winter when my husband, Louis, left me alone for the first time — he had to check his trapline. Suddenly the wonderful, wide, white outdoor refrigerator that had been freezing my nine varieties of sherbets and ice cream turned into a hostile, stealthy, ghostly silence. I gulped at my diminishing courage.

By four o'clock of the first day of Louis's absence, when darkness obliterated the last ray of daylight, I was in panic. With the temperature at 35 degrees below zero, the cabin was popping as the cold gripped it, the lake was booming, and the river groaning and grinding. The restless howling of the huskies didn't help. I stuck my head out the door to yell "shut up" but the words froze in my throat.

The huskies were responding to the nearby howling of wolves - and these wolves didn't sound at all like they did on the records enthralled city naturalists played. It sounded to me as if they were meditating on killing; and my new husband was out there, probably in the midst of the pack, with only a single shot .22 Remington. If I didn't want to be a widow, I'd have to rescue him with my .270 Winchester.

I had only a vague idea of the direction Louis had gone. I had

56

never been on snowshoes, but I knew from watching television that it would be easy to hike off through the deep woods wearing the big webs. I found an old pair that belonged to Louis and, with plenty of rope wrapped around the frame and my feet, I was able to start. But between unravelling my feet and digging myself out of snowbanks I wasn't exactly eating up the miles. I soon realized I'd be lucky to get back to the cabin.

It was a miracle that I did get back because the cabin seemed to have moved in the time since I had left it. But I was far from licked! My husband had to be saved from those wolves!

I grabbed a can of oil and poured it on the first building I found in the darkness. It made a beautiful fire that was very comforting to my city-bred eyes, and I returned to the cabin to draw a comfortable chair up to the window to enjoy it. I was sure that it was guiding my husband to safety. I was drowsing in my chair when the cabin door flew open and Louis rushed in yelling: "The outhouse is on fire."

I flung my arms around him blubbering: "You're not dead. They didn't kill you!"

"Who in hell was going to kill me?"

"Wolves!"

Since the tone of his voice sounded reprimanding, I thought I'd better make my story good, so I finished rather breathlessly: "And they were trying to crawl through the windows."

Louis gave me a queer look, grabbed a lantern and headed out the door. "Come on, let's look at their tracks."

Tracks? I hadn't thought of tracks. I dragged behind Louis as, head down and lantern high, he searched the snow around the cabin. Suddenly I pointed. "There. Wolf tracks."

"Dog," Louis grunted, heading back to the cabin. Inside he grabbed me by the shoulders. "When I heard those wolves I had a damn good hunch I'd better get back and check up on my city wife. Of course there are wolves out there. You've got to remember that I'm a trapper."

"And that animals leave tracks," I mumbled under my breath.

It wasn't long before Louis brought in a day's catch — four lynx, six marten, and one mink. I was aghast. "You can't hang them around the stove. I've got to cook."

"Of course I have to hang them here. I can't skin them until they're thawed."

In the night MiMi, my little silver French poodle, woke me with her scratching. Annabel, the cat, was scratching. Louis, still asleep, also was scratching. Then I felt a bing, sting, bite. I jabbed Louis in the ribs. "Louis, something is biting me."

With a groan Louis rolled over. "I suppose those lynx have fleas."

"Ouch. Louis, you'll have to throw those lynx out."

"I can't until I skin them."

"You'll have to do something. Ouch. "

We rolled out of bed and Louis threw back the covers. Tiny black specks were jumping all over the white sheets. "How could anything that small bite so hard?" I wanted to know.

"They sure must make life hell for the lynx."

Trying not to make it sound like an ultimatum I suggested: "Don't you think it would be better if you built a shed onto the cabin for your furs?"

"Yeah, I guess it's not such a good idea to bring my catch into the same room where we eat, sleep, and cook."

A few days later we were eating breakfast when I was delighted to see a squirrel skip over the snow, climb a stump, and eat some nuts I had put there for him. Since our nearest friends were more than 20 miles away, I treasured the squirrel. But suddenly Louis saw the squirrel. He leaped up and dashed outside with his .22 rifle, and abruptly the squirrel plummeted backward into the snow. With a beaming face Louis grabbed it by the tail and stomped back into the cabin.

"I've just earned a dollar."

I looked at him, horrified. Had I married a barbarian?

"You're a brute," I shrieked.

"I'm a trapper. How do you think you're going to continue to eat the ham and eggs you seem to be enjoying if I don't catch fur? Besides, squirrels are the worst pests in the woods."

"I don't believe it."

"You'll find out, dear wife, you'll find out."

I did find out within a short time when a squirrel ate the hem out of my new muskrat coat, chewed up a stored mattress, then demolished multiple things edible and nonedible in one of our caches.

Nevertheless, from that day to this, one-half mile around our trapping cabin has been designated as a sanctuary for furbearers. Soon, almost every evening a fox came into the yard to tease the huskies and to get the frozen fish I tossed to him. He never seemed to tire of flipping the fish into the air then deftly catching it. Then an otter appropriated our water hole. He would struggle up the bank then slide into the water with all the grace of a ski pro. I often wondered how much chlorine government officials would consider necessary for our drinking water after the otter had bathed in it.

One morning we awoke to find the spot where eight wolves had slept almost against the back cabin wall. On another morning we found a moose sleeping in our small potato patch.

However, not all was paradise in our sanctuary. The fox gave me anxious moments when he was about while grouse were buried in the snow for warmth. Great horned owls, hooting their deep mysterious calls, not only gave me thrills but chills when I saw where their broad wings had brushed the snow as they swooped down upon some unsuspecting snowshoe hare. I dreaded the terrified screech of squirrels being pursued by marten through the upper branches of the surrounding spruce forest. But the terror of a wolf pack in full cry, bloodthirsty to kill, was the most horrible of all, for I soon learned that they don't kill quickly and cleanly. Their prey often dies in agony as the pack eats it alive, bite by savage bite.

Living on a trapline does have its rewards. Once we returned from a trip to find every tree, willow bush, woodpile, fence, and even our cabin roof occupied by roosting sharptailed grouse. They awakened in me an elated realization of how fortunate I was to share this wonderful earth with other creatures. Each spring the mating calls and dances of the sharptails in the wild meadow below our cabin give us a wonderful lift of spirit after our seven-month winter. Our Indian friends here tell us that a little owl wakes up spring and tells the sharptails it is time for their dancing ceremonies. Never has the plaintive "wiloo, wiloo" call failed to bring to mind the fragrance of wild flowers, fresh earth, and the exhilarating expectancy of spring — even when it is snowing.

The shift from noisy, crowded city to quiet, isolated solitude almost drove me crazy. Without movies, television, and other entertainment I felt lost. I missed the neon signs and the bright glow from millions of electric lights. At first my ambition was to buy hundreds of strings of lights and wrap them around every tree and bush surrounding our cabin. Today I realize how artificial electric lights are and I couldn't stand to have them blotting out the beauty of our fantastic northern sky.

When the sun hid from us for almost two months, far across the lake and behind the mountains, I felt almost as if I was groping around in a cave. I decided that two small windows in a cabin were not enough, but Louis balked at one of my suggestions to remedy it. "Who ever heard of picture windows in a trapper's cabin?"

In due time two large crates arrived with the picture windows, and Louis leaned them against the back of the cabin after building a makeshift roof for their protection. Installation had to wait until the warmer weather of spring.

A few days after the windows had arrived we awoke to blood curdling screeching, blowing, and hissing. A loose husky was rampaging hysterically around the outside of the cabin. Louis grabbed for his pants and snatched up his .22 rifle saying, unnecessarily: "Something's up."

As he reached the yard the husky gave a howl of injury and Louis yelled: "Something's back here."

I peeked out of the window and saw Louis pointing his rifle at my new windows. I leaped out of bed and, not bothering with slippers, rushed out the door in nightgown and bare feet, screaming at Louis: "Stop, stop. The windows."

"I'm not aiming at the damned windows," Louis swore, thinking only of the cabin windows.

"Yes, you are. Stop," I screamed, hopping up and down with my bare feet in the snow. The dog raced past, roaring in frustration.

There was a four-inch space between the two window crates and from the depths of this crack came a chilling series of roars and hisses. Louis, with a set jaw, again took careful aim. I covered my ears, expecting to hear a tremendous crash as my four-and-a-half-by-five foot windows flew into splinters. "Crack," went the rifle. I groaned and grabbed a foot that was freezing.

"Hit him," Louis beamed. "All I could see was a little white mark." There was no more hissing. Louis motioned, "Hold this crate to the side so I can crawl in and get him."

I was not only freezing from the cold, but from the thought of groping around in the winter darkness for the rest of my life, for I was sure the bullet had gone through the animal and the glass.

Louis puffed back out elated, holding up a mink. "Look. That shot stuck right here in his throat and never went through. That was sure a lucky shot."

"Lucky," I whispered, feeling faint from the strain. "Thank God there will be light."

There was never a gloomier approach to Christmas than my first year in the North. How could there be Christmas without Santa Claus, bells ringing in the streets, and gigantic store windows displaying all the wonders of a prosperous nation?

I needed shops filled with Christmas candy, or a 35-foot Christmas tree with all its twinkling and blinking colored lights. What is Christmassy about a Yukon trapline? Nothing. There wasn't even a gift, for we hadn't been to town since the first of September. There wouldn't even be a stuffed toy to add to my collection.

In previous years on more distant traplines, Christmas had come and gone unnoticed by my husband, but to cheer up his new wife he harnessed the dog team and we took off after a perfect Christmas tree. It looked hopeless. Because of the sub-arctic climate, most trees in the region lack symmetry. Finally the huskies became tired of the monkey business and dumped us under an almost perfect tree.

I did cheer up a little on our return, for the tree smelled like all of the Christmas trees I had ever known, and I noticed that the bells on the dog team jingled like Santa's bells on the street at home. We decorated the tree with unravelled red yarn from a pair of Louis' wool socks, blue yarn from a sweater, and shiny gold and silver fishing lure spinners.

Louis was tired Christmas Eve and went to bed early, leaving me to stare at the giftless and lonesome-looking tree. Finally I could no longer stand it and rushed out of the cabin into the outdoors where I could let loose all my pent-up despair. I took a big breath to burst into tears, but instead I held my breath with awe. Above me a vast panorama of waving curtains of northern lights spread across the entire sky. Our little stove pipe billowed smoke up into a brilliant dazzling arch of pink and green. Above the doghouses curled and snaked a whip of yellow fire, and straight overhead, like fireworks, rained down showers of purple and lavender flares. I suddenly realized that no man-made department store or array of neon lights could possibly match this glorious display.

After I had watched the amazing display above for a long time the dogs softly woofed, and I looked to see what they had seen. A stately moose stalked into sight, dark amidst the sparkling snow. It was a regular Christmas card scene, I thought. And then the truth dawned: I really lived on a Christmas card.

Louis was awake when I returned to the cabin with my spirits soaring. "I wondered when you would come back. You've been moaning that you would have no stuffed animal toy for Christmas. What do you think of that?" Following his pointed finger to the Christmas tree I first saw only green branches.

"Keep looking," Louis insisted.

The tree quivered, then suddenly I saw peeking around the trunk a tiny white head and two beady black eyes. I was delighted.

"Whatever is it?" I asked.

"Be patient and keep still. He'll soon start his acrobatics."

"Is it a mouse?" I whispered.

"Absolutely not," Louis laughed.

The tree started to shake as a little white streak frisked to the very top, watching us with interest, flicking a black-tipped tail. "An ermine!" I gasped.

Frightened at my exclamation, he dashed from branch to branch and raced up and down the trunk. "Well?" Louis asked. "Isn't that better than your manufactured stuffed toy?"

"He's going to have to have a name," I suggested.

"How about Archibald?" Louis joked.

"Not for such a tiny animal."

"Well then, Timmy."

"Perfect," I agreed.

Next morning, Timmy was peeking at us from the centre overhead beam of the cabin. If we stirred he frisked back out the air vent, but was back in no time prospecting for a meal. He was a joy to have around, and soon became quite tame. He proved to be the best mousetrap ever and with him around we no longer had trouble from mice. But we did have trouble with Timmy's appetite. Our frozen fish began to disappear at an alarming rate and mysterious holes appeared in our frozen moose meat. That was bad enough, but when he found our few precious fresh carrots and potatoes it was a disaster. To save some for ourselves we had to put them into tins. Only when a marten moved into the cache near our cabin did Timmy's foraging trips slow down.

In January of my first year as a trapper's wife I discovered my greatest enemy was not the remote, isolated North. In fact, my main foes came from Japan, Italy, France, England, and Germany. They were the fur buyers who congregated in the Canadian cities where the big fur auctions are held.

It was when five very light, beautiful lynx skins I was hoarding for a parka disappeared into a gunny sack tagged for a Toronto auction that I fully realized the fur buyers and I were in for years of tug-of-war. Bidding at fur auctions is guided by the caprice of fashion. If in one year Louis caught mostly short-haired fur, the fashion was sure to be for long-haired furs like wolf, fox, lynx and wolverine — pushing the prices for marten, otter, muskrat, squirrel, beaver and mink so low we ate beans. (But then, beans with moose meat isn't so bad.)

When I visit in the Lower 48 and see society women and skinny fashion models wearing fur coats I grit my teeth. But for them, I too would have a mink coat, a fox stole, and a lynx parka. I sure need it more than most, for here in the Yukon our winter temperatures have zoomed down to -82 degrees. If we have a winter with temperatures no colder than -50 we think we are practically having a heat wave.

One winter, when the price of lynx furs had soared to the unheard-of heights of $600, we had a lovely shaded lynx come into the yard to tease the dogs at night. The dogs became almost frantic, and we didn't get much sleep. In time the lynx became so bold that he came to the cabin in full daylight, He looked to be a big cuddly lovable cat, fluffy and innocent-eyed. He would sit for hours watching our activities, not realizing he sat in a protected zone, saving his hide and preventing us from collecting $600.

Then a larger tom moved into the area, and by the time he was through with our regular visitor that animal's fur wasn't worth throwing away. We cooked his carcass for the dogs. The big killer tom went on to kill several other lynx kittens we were aware of nearby.

One morning, when Louis was working his way through a stack of sourdough hotcakes, he asked rather urgently: "Where's the butter?"

"I'm sorry, but the marten stole the last pound of butter we had," I apologized.

"A whole pound?" Louis roared. "I can't believe it."

"If you don't believe it, track him down. Maybe he left enough for your hotcakes," I suggested.

"I sure will," Louis said as he took off. Soon he came back holding a thin butter wrapper, empty. "I'll trap that son-of-a-gun," he threatened.

"Oh no you won't. Not here. It's protected territory. Don't you forget it," I reminded him.

"Yeah, but I killed the mink here," he reminded me.

"I'm afraid the law enforcer was under duress at the time. It was a slip."

Louis groaned and muttered threats about what he would do to the marten that stole butter. He cut a slice of moose meat and slammed it onto his plate just as Timmy bounced onto the table. Timmy sat at the edge of Louis' plate eying the slice of meat, then he started emitting sounds challenging Louis' right to that slice of meat. He sounded so ferocious that I had to smother a laugh, and Louis, startled, leaned back out of reach of the tiny weasel's white teeth.

Timmy made a grab and starting tugging at the meat. As he watched part of his breakfast slowly move off his plate, an amused Louis blustered: "What's going on around here? I'm supposed to be a trapper."

"Dear," I giggled, "you're just being tamed."

Two big game outfitters, Louis and Dolores, on the trail to the Snake River, near the Arctic Circle and Northwest Territories.

Louis freighting trophies on the Bonnet Plume River.

Dolores and Zitzie, her favorite husky, on the Bonnet Plume.

Dolores with three of her chief guides: Harry Baum, Lonny Johnny, and Harry McGinty.

Above: Louis shoeing horses with wrangler Jimmy Johnny.

Right: Dolores with guide Paul Germain freighting supplies on Fairchild Lake.

Left: Dolores cooking breakfast over a campfire.

Below: Dolores with guide Lonny Johnny in the tent the grizzly wrecked.

Above: Pack train traveling along Dolores Lake on the Bonnet Plume.

Left: Dolores in patch of wild flowers in the high pass on the way to Wind River.

Dolores with hunter and caribou.

Dolores having tea with her staff of Indian guides.

Dolores sorting supplies at the Bonnet Plume cache.

Packing and repacking—an art and essential skill on the trail.

Louis leading pack train across the Bonnet Plume River.

Louis proudly shows a beautiful Dall ram.

What's left after three grizzlies investigated Dolores's kitchen. All the stainless steel pans had tooth holes.

Dolores and Swiss hunter, Miss Nobholts, with her record moose now on display in Salzberg.

Dolores, with staff of Indian guides, holding Zitzie.

Headed for camp crossing on the Bonnet Plume River.

Louis prospecting on hunting area.

Chief guide Harry Baum with caribou horns.

Dolores with four of her Swiss hunters having breakfast

Louis with wolf kicked out of the pack and eating Highland beef.

Dolores and Louis with record Dall ram.

77

Dolores waking up on a winter trail.

Dolores at the supply
cabin's bear door.

Dolores using makeup on the trophy trail.

Guides looking over hunting country of Castle mountains.

Louis with Yukon grizzly.

Louis and Dolores with the horns of two moose grizzlies had killed.

79

Dolores on cache a grizzly had kept her up on all night.

Dolores repacking horse that had run over a bees' nest.

Pack train on the way to the high country.

Above: Browns' log cabin home in the Yukon.

Left: Dolores in the basement of their home with a winter's supply of meat.

Below: Raising turkeys at the ranch.

Part of Louis's herd of
Scotch Highlanders.

Right: Dolores's French
bedroom in the bush.

Guides skin out the grizzly that kept Dolores on the cache all night.

Dolores with their bush pilot, Chuck.

Raising chickens at -78°F was sometimes difficult.

Pack train.

Louis loaded for a winter trip to his hunting area.

Louis with Kate, one of his favorite riding horses.

Pack train traveling through pass in late fall.

Dolores and Louis picking wild roses and blue chiming bells.

Chief cook and bottle washer
baking pies on the hunt.

Dolores and Louis enjoying
a quiet moment.

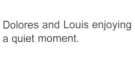

Chapter 10

HEADING FOR THE BUSH OR YOUR GRAVE?

(By Louis Brown)

It looks to me as if the government agencies adding huge areas of wilderness to their domain might be in for a shock to learn that, instead of creating recreational areas, they may be turning the North into a vast graveyard.

Since 1934 I've lived as a trapper, guide and big game outfitter in the remote wilderness of Yukon Territory, Canada. Until recently it wasn't unusual for me to see no human face but my own in the mirror for a year or even two. You can't live that long in the bush without having a few close encounters with the Grim Reaper, so I thought I knew all the ways one could kill himself in the great outdoors. But in the last few years a new breed has invaded the Yukon and they have shown us old-timers newfangled ways of getting killed that I thought could only be dreamed up by Alfred Hitchcock.

Yearly our landscape gets more cluttered with makeshift crosses planted next to dangerous rapids, rough rock tombstones piled on sides of mountains, and posts with grim epitaphs stuck in surprising places. It sure takes the pleasure out of viewing the scenery with these reminders of death in the way. Nine times out of ten, these deaths could have been prevented with proper knowledge — or just common sense.

You can't gain wilderness savvy by reading books and articles written by people who dash through the bush for a month or two and then, because they came out alive, pose as experts on the great outdoors and hand out advice that would make Davy Crockett turn over in his grave.

Even some who should know better give advice that scares the hell out of me. For example, in her book, Arctic Wild, Lois Crisler rocked me back in my chair when she claimed she used a couple of

89

secret weapons on grizzly bears. One was the element of surprise. My God, how many Yukoners lie under the frostline now because they surprised a grizzly? Even worse, she describes her other secret weapon as a bear rattle made of a two-and-a-half-pound can with an empty evaporated milk can and a couple of pebbles inside. If it had been an irritable grizzly that she surprised, Lois's bones would have been rattling — not the cans.

A woodcutter working for Harry Francis here in the Yukon had the same idea. He was warned several times by trapper friends to get rid of a large grizzly hanging around his camp, but the woodcutter assured his friends he was safe, for he always carried a can of rocks and if the bear came close he rattled the can.

One day his friends arrived for a visit to find only a few uneaten parts of the woodcutter. They gathered the remains, put them in the old cabin and hurried to report to the RCMP. When they returned with the police they found that the grizzly had broken into the cabin and finished his meal.

On three different occasions that I personally know about, Barren Ground grizzlies were hellbent on exterminating a 20-man camp bustling with activity. Where would Lois be rattling her little can of rocks with a bear in such a mood?

Theories can kill. You're probably asking, "if I can't depend on books, what can I depend on?" I say, depend upon yourself. But until you get enough firsthand experience to have the answers, go to a real old-timer with years and years of bush savvy in the area you're interested in. That's what I did when I first came into the country, and I learned things that are never found in books.

Someone once said: "The human mind has a terrific capacity for resisting information." Today a cross stuck in the ground beside Five Mile Rapids on the Stewart River proves that statement was made by a man who understood human nature. On one of my trips to town I heard old timers talking about the couple from Outside who had ignored all their advice about tackling the Stewart River in flood with the type of equipment they had. I used to love the challenge and thrill of running Five Mile Rapids until that cross got stuck there. Now all I can think of is some geezer saying: "The stupidity of man is limitless."

To cap that experience, last June a young fellow arrived at our house dripping wet. My wife, Dolores, almost fainted, and I felt like giving him hell when he told us he had just swum across the Stewart River on an inner tube. The temperature of the Stewart in June is about two degrees above freezing, and the river is wide. The boy said that, before he reached our side of the river, he could barely move his hands because of the cold. If the current had kept him from shore for any time he'd have never made it. Hypothermia and drowning would have killed him.

A local government authority had heard about this kid and tried to catch him before he attempted his swim — the government man knew the great expense of dragging that river for a body.

Unfortunately, too many dreamers are leaving the asphalt jungles to: "conquer the wilderness". Such an approach shuts an old-timer up tighter than a clam. It would pay for many of those who arrive in the bush flaunting their college degrees to reassess the nature of knowledge: a sod roof and an outhouse do not always indicate that a place is occupied by a moron. A man who lives in this style usually does so because he wants to, and he could give a city dweller advice that could keep him out of a lot of trouble or even, quite simply, save his life.

I recently read an adventure account of a young man who had himself flown into wilderness Alaska so he could hike out. He was overloaded with gear he didn't need, he ran out of food, he couldn't follow his map and he got lost. He was near starvation when someone happened across him. Adventure, hell! For any old-timer or young-timer with common sense, such a trip would have been an uneventful, everyday occurrence. But this guy did everything wrong and called it adventure. The area he hiked across (it was summer too — the easy time of year) is now designated as a national monument, and I expect others from big cities to follow his "adventurous" ways. In recent years, many former big city residents have arrived in Alaska and the Yukon, arranged for use of a remote cabin and had themselves flown in to spend the winter. In one instance an individual, living alone, ran out of food in mid winter and put out an SOS that a passing plane saw. Another froze to death on the trail when he tried to travel in -50°F temperatures. Others have run out of firewood. One partnership of two men broke up when cabin fever erupted in midwinter after the two had remained inside, afraid to venture into the cold, for weeks on end.

A few years ago one of the top outdoor magazines ran a series of survival articles covering everything from the kind of gun to buy to what kind of pants not to buy for wilderness living. Not one word was written about the mental attitude necessary for survival. That was a major omission, and here's why I think so.

A short time before Dolores and I retired from the big game out-

91

fitting business here in the Yukon, we were camped in high country in August when a blizzard suddenly hit. My chief guide, an experienced Indian hunter-trapper, came running to see me. "Boss, that hunter with big glasses is actin' crazy," he reported.

I agreed to go check, thinking there was some little misunderstanding. At first I couldn't make heads or tails out of the hunter's blubbering. I finally caught the words, ". . . freezing to death . . . lost and never found."

I reassured him. "There's no danger. You can always expect snow in high country at this time of year this Far North."

The man then lost all control. He screamed and hurled obscenities at me, at the snow, at the wind, the mountains, the Indian guides. Even when it stopped snowing he was sure he wasn't going to survive.

On the last hunt of that year our cook tent burned down. We had a new cook tent and plenty of grub in the cache, so there was no emergency, but when the hunter rode into camp and saw the smoking tent he went into hysterics, wringing his hands, pacing up and down - and a mule skinner couldn't have blasphemed with more pungency. For three days, until we got him on a plane out of there, the lot of us — guides and outfitter alike — were destined for a warm eternity if he had his way. Trailing the packtrain home, the guides and I held a post-mortem on the hunt. My guides were full-blooded Indians and some had never been to school, but they were smart and I valued their opinions. They could size up a hunter in one second flat. Their psychological evaluation of the two hunters we had just had flabbergasted me. They told me something I wouldn't have thought of in a hundred years.

Lonny shook his head: "All the time TV, and more TV. They did not see anything here. Just talked TV," was his view of the hunters.

"Now Lonny," I remonstrated, "They were both on some pretty tough but successful hunts. That one got a tiger in India, and..."

The guides roared with laughter. Lonny bent double with mirth. "That man on the first hunt told us all about a tiger hunt on TV."

Johnson summed up their views. "Those guys are TV-crazy in the head."

I grew clammy thinking about it. Could a man get so mixed up he took, or I should say, mistook a TV adventure for reality? Yes, says prominent scientist Jerry Manders in his book Four Arguments for the Elimination of TV. He hit it plumb centre when he wrote that people were confusing television experience with direct experience. More and more TV is becoming the reality while the world around us is the unreality. That makes a situation more mixed up than scrambled eggs.

Say a TV producer dreams up an African safari with all the excitement, thrills, shooting and success. By the time the show is over the viewer thinks he knows hunting from A to Z. He feels equal to tackling the toughest hunt. In truth he feels he could show those brawny guides a thing or two. There you have the situation of confusing TV experience with direct experience. When he hotfoots it to book a hunt, it never occurs to him the TV experience hasn't toughened his muscles, built up his stamina, or mentally conditioned him for hardships. If any unexpected event disturbs his placid, TV-conditioned mind he can't cope. Banging up against a direct experience, he goes to pieces.

There are also the characters who arrive in the North and, when warned of dangers, say: "It's none of your business if we hit for the bush and get lost."

The hell it isn't! It's our business when we have to pay for that plane or chopper to hunt for their carcasses. Rescues made by the government — our taxes — are expensive.

A man who has made up his mind to hit the bush should prepare himself in every possible way. He should not forget that Mother Nature holds a million tricks up her sleeve and that no one ever learns them all. She can hand you a joker at any time. For example, who would have thought that tough, woods-wise, born-and-raised on-a-Yukon-trapline Eddy Wilkenson could have been killed by a grizzly in the dead of winter and that his body would be eaten by a pack of wolves? The bear that killed him should have been holed up in hibernation. Eddy knew that bears wandering around in midwinter are the most dangerous kind. What he didn't know was that such a bear was near his cabin, and he went out without a rifle, probably thinking he was going to retrieve a marten from a nearby trap.

No one can always be prepared.

To me, what is even more irresponsible is the fairly common occurrence of ignorant and inexperienced adults stumbling around the bush with their small children. In recent years we've had a number of cases of babies having their little hands and feet frozen. One child was found frozen dead under a tree. Sound impossible? If you have doubts, write to Dr. J.V. Clark, of Mayo, Yukon Territory. If he's in good form he'll spell out what kind of city people have been arriving to "conquer the wilderness" in recent years. Sure there have been thousands of kids raised in the bush, but I'll leave it to you to figure out what kind of parents they had. An old-timer once told me the type of man he felt best suited for the bush: "A happy man with no chip on his shoulder, who never holds a grudge, and who never gets moody."

What happens when a moody man goes into the bush? Ted Skonsen, one of the co-discoverers of Anvil zinc and lead mines at Ross River, here in the Yukon, could tell you. Before Ted took up prospecting, a big strong Finn talked him into going trapping with him up the South Fork of the Hess River. Ted hadn't heard that the Finn was OK as long as he was around people, but that after a few weeks in the bush he grew moody.

Ted awoke one morning to the sudden realization that he was more than 200 miles from help, alone with a crazy. Cunningly, the Finn had hidden all the guns, axes and knives before he fastened a dog chain around Ted's neck and told him, "Mush. You're my dog now. You work like hell or I kill."

When Ted tried to break away, the Finn knifed him. I've seen the scars on his face. Ted lived a life of hell for a few weeks before he managed to get the Finn back down the 200-mile trail to Mayo.

The list of names of men who have become disconnected while isolated in the bush here in the North is like a roll call of Satan's demons.

The best of Ripley's Believe It or Not has never been written. Unbelievable things are happening all the time here, nowadays. For example, a man and woman were recently seen heading for the bush with nothing more than a 50-pound sack of carrots for supplies, and they apparently had nothing more serious on their minds than Yoga.

I guess Robert Service came close when he said something about the North not being won by weaklings, but by men with hearts of Vikings. That's fine, of course, but if you have the heart of a Viking, and plan to survive in the North, you'd still better check your plans with an old-timer. What he tells you could save your life.

Chapter 11

GRIZZLY IN MY GREENHOUSE?

When you live in the middle of one of Yukon Territory's finest big game areas, anything can happen. We're used to grizzlies sleeping on our haystacks, wolves chasing our cats up trees, moose knocking down our fences and great horned owls plugging up our stovepipe, but we weren't prepared for what happened one April.

Under waving banners of northern lights, my husband, Louis, and I were returning from a shopping trip to Whitehorse. We were anxious to get home to check on our maternity ward of seven registered Scotch Highland cows and their two-day- to two-week-old calves. I was also anxious about my plastic-covered greenhouse. In February I had planted tomato and cucumber seeds in the house and had just transplanted the tender six-inch plants to the greenhouse after Louis patched a large hole in the plastic. I had issued an ultimatum. "Louis, if any of your old cows poke more holes in my greenhouse, I'm going to chase them out of the ranch yard."

Taku, my big, wolf-grey Siberian husky, met us at the gate, dragging his chain. We knew trouble was brewing. We've never been able to trust our huskies with our cattle. Once, Zitzie, another husky, broke loose and in about five seconds had a calf down by the throat. Louis had reasons when he said, "Hell, I wonder how many calves he's eaten."

When I opened the gate, Taku slunk guiltily to me knowing he had no business being loose. He was covered with blood, one eye was swollen shut and his face was badly slashed, as if something sharp had raked him. At the thought of a cow mauling Taku's face so badly while defending her calf, I felt suddenly sick.

Louis ran to where the bawling cows were bunched together. He returned, smiling broadly. "Taku must not be hungry. They are all here.

I wonder what's upsetting them. Never seen them so skittish, even when a husky is loose."

Even Blazer, our bull, was nervously pacing on the other side of the fence where he had been relegated after challenging my possession of the outhouse.

Assured the cattle were safe, I inspected the greenhouse. Rounding the corner I stopped in dismay, wondering whether I should howl with rage or cry my eyes out. Through a large jagged hole, I saw my tomato and cucumber plants sagging under a drift of snow blown in through the opening. I sputtered: "You better get your old cows out of here before they wreck the place."

Louis examined the torn plastic and gave a puzzled grunt, "Looks to me like claw marks around the hole. Do you suppose Taku could have done this?"

"Taku after tomato plants? Don't be silly."

"Don't forget, you hung a slab of tallow in there to keep it safe from varmints."

It was true. I was saving the tallow to try making some fancy French soap. Louis jerked the door of the greenhouse open, then laughed, "You can forget about your soap unless you want to render out Taku's hide."

"If we hurry maybe we can save my plants," I urged. While I built a fire and brushed snow from the tiny plants, Louis patched the plastic for the second time.

Tying Taku securely to his wire run, we went to the house to be greeted by my 10-pound silver-grey French poodle, who leaped and yipped her joy. MiMi is a big part of our ranch. She bosses the huskies and has several times bluffed the bull out of the yard by fearlessly hanging onto his tail.

I was exhausted. Starting out at 3am under a million icy, sparkling stars to get to Whitehorse in time to start shopping when the stores opened, rushing to buy for horses, cows, chickens and ourselves until the stores closed at 5:30pm, then driving back home to conclude our 500 mile round trip drained every drop of our energy.

We were getting ready for bed when Taku started barking furiously. Taku has several kinds of barks. He uses an excited bark for an approaching car and a warning bark for a trespassing cow, but when he's barking as he did then he means business and he wants us to hurry.

I jammed feet into fur slippers, and as I raced out the back door, grabbed my Winchester .270, a part of my kitchen equipment which I keep beside the spice rack. Taku was tied about 75 feet from the back porch and I could see he was looking toward the hutches of my white Angora rabbits. THUMP... THUMP . . . THUMP. Blocky, the buck, was giving the intruder dire warning. I yelled, "get out of here, get out," then tumbled into bed.

We hadn't had time to close our eyes when Taku went into hysterics. I was out the door before Louis could find his shoes. Taku was looking straight at me. In disgust I yelled at him, "look at the varmint, not me, so I can tell where he is."

The next moment my permanent straightened. A huge black hulk rose beside me not eight feet away. I fell back through the kitchen door and with all haste helped my husband find his other shoe.

Louis snatched up his .308 lever action Savage and dashed out the door, skidding on the varmint's calling card and falling off the porch. Something hit the barbed-wire fence with a "zing" and we could hear a heavy body run down the 80-foot embankment to the frozen lake.

Our log cabin sits on a high bench overlooking a sheltered lake rimmed with spruce and birch trees. In summer it's a haven for Canada honkers, wild ducks and swans. However, for seven months the only signs of life on its frozen surface are usually muskrat houses and wolf tracks. Louis picked himself up, muttered a few unprintable epithets, and grunted wearily: "It's a bear, most likely black, and now we've scared hell out of him, let's get some sleep."

We had just pulled the covers over us when MiMi started yipping. We both erupted out of bed. Taku was frantic. I glanced out the window in time to see the rear end of something big back out through the side of the greenhouse. By the time we reached the greenhouse, nothing was there but another large hole. Suddenly, Taku's barking changed; he was telling us that he was about to be slaughtered. Louis raced over and stopped in front of a spruce tree to peer down the bank. On the other side of the tree, Taku leaped and snarled at the end of his wire run.

I dashed to the house and grabbed my 9x35 power binoculars. Standing on the back porch, I focused the glasses on Taku. His jaws were viciously snapping at something down the bank. Shifting the glasses slightly, I caught my breath. A huge, dark, menacing head loomed over the bank inches from Taku's gleaming fangs. Slowly, a big hump rose. It was a grizzly.

Six feet of spreading evergreen branches separated Louis from the bear. I was afraid to yell a warning for fear the grizzly would charge.

In the dim light, I was afraid to shoot. A heart shot was no good at such close quarters. For years Louis and our Indian guides have coached me always to aim to break down a bear's front quarters in a tight spot.

I saw the grizzly raise his paw to bat Taku, and the enraged husky grabbed it. I was so excited I screamed "GRIZZLY!" before I could think.

Louis sprinted around the spruce just as the grizzly dashed down the bank through the brush. The cows and calves were wildly running in all directions. I ran to the edge of the bank. I knew Louis would be unable to see the grizzly from where he was, but I caught a glimpse of the bear as he stood for a moment on a patch of snow. I raised my gun and leaned over to clear a stubby birch tree. My left foot slipped on a crust of snow and the rifle flew out of my hands while I tobogganed down through prickly wild rose bushes, slamming to a stop against an old stump.

Louis yelled: "Get back up here quick. Blazer has knocked down the fence. Get in the house."

Either Blazer's bellows were shaking the ground or my knees were vibrating. Louis took off, running along the top of the bench. I glanced down and saw a dark shadow. The grizzly was climbing up the trail that would bring him to the corrals where there were two pregnant cows.

Terrified for fear Blazer might charge down the bank, I started to slide all the way down and climb a tree when I realized I'd be leaving Louis alone with the grizzly. Desperately clawing and scratching my way back up the bank, I felt as if my wildly pounding heart was plugging my breathing apparatus and I gasped for breath.

Blazer, infuriated by the grizzly smell, was pawing at the dirt and snow and tearing up the ground with his horns. I didn't dare pass him to go to the corrals, where I was sure Louis had gone. Horrified, I saw the bull hook a wool shirt from the clothesline and pulverize it. It took little imagination to picture what would happen to anyone inside the shirt.

Just then the cows and calves stampeded out through the hole Blazer had made in the fence. If they fled down the trail, there was sure to be an explosive meeting with the grizzly.

I dashed to the house for a warmer coat. MiMi, highly excited by all the noise, ran out between my legs. With one look at Blazer, her personal enemy, she took after him. Blazer fled in terror from MiMi's ferocious yipping. She trotted back, with a self-satisfied look.

I started for the corrals, avoiding the bull by staying among the trees. Through the dim light, I finally saw Louis standing by the log corral. I crept up to him. He motioned toward the dark timber. Breathlessly, we waited.

I kept wishing the grizzly would go away. Although they have scared me until my teeth rattled, I still love the big brutes. In the 17 years I've been on the big game trails, they have come into our camp 13 times. They have chased me up onto caches, then spent all night trying to knock me down. They have stood on their hind legs about 12 feet from me when I had no gun and looked me over. They have paced the outer rim of my campfire when as I sat alone clutching my gun. In spite of the grey hairs and insomnia they have given me, I have only admiration for the grizzly.

Louis nudged me and I saw a dark hulk emerge from the shadows. The grizzly came straight for the corrals. I thought, "oh, go back, go back," but it has been my experience that no noise or light will stop a determined grizzly.

The light rubber scope protector on Louis's rifle gently tapped against the barrel. The grizzly stopped. How keen was his hearing! He spotted us, then charged. Louis raised his rifle and fired once, and the grizzly crumbled, never to move again. Louis murmured, "too bad, old fellow."

"Let's get back to bed and get some sleep," Louis suggested.

"Not before you patch my greenhouse. You won't have to do it again," I coaxed. The sun was rosy red before we finished the patching. While we were eating sourdough hotcakes I said: "You owe Taku an apology for accusing him of making the holes in my greenhouse." Louis snorted: "Taku is lucky he isn't a dead dog."

Chapter 12

WHY OUTFITTERS GET GREY

We were in taboo country about seventy miles south of the Arctic Circle, but farther north in central Yukon than I had ever hunted. My big game party was camped in a place the Indians strictly avoided even before the advent of whites. Here was supposed to be the fiercest and largest of animals — a spotted wolf so savage that you are dead before bow and arrow can be raised. The grizzlies here are reputed to be cunning trackers of men. So warned my Indian guides.

Our tents fronted a dry wash leading to a shallow, unnamed stream. Behind were stunted Arctic spruce no higher than a grizzly can reach. A few willows straggled along the bank.

I had sent the hunters with their guides out on a fly trip after grizzly, and kept the wrangler with me to supply wood for the cookstove. The bread, cake, and pie box was empty and I set out to replenish it.

Alec Johnny was only 14 years old, but because of his love for horses he was one of our best wranglers. He could track down a wanted horse in a maze of other tracks, a talent inherited from his dad, who was employed for many years on my husband's staff of Indian guides.

I had just sent Alec out to round up a stray horse and was elbow deep in bread dough when a loud, rumbling roar vibrated between the mountain ridges. I couldn't decide what animal had made the terrifying sound. Another bawling roar and I yanked my hands out of the dough, grabbed my rifle, and ran to the middle of the dry wash.

I could see nothing from there, so ran toward the stream. The bellowing was getting louder and closer. Rounding a clump of willows, I saw three gigantic grizzlies on the other side of the shallow stream. My Winchester .270 was loaded, but it held only five shells. I knew there wasn't a chance in Hades I could kill three grizzlies with five shots, and there was no time to hunt for more shells among the dozen or more pack boxes. Even if I could kill the bears, the hunters would certainly raise hell if they returned with no grizzly and I had three.

I placed a shot in the water, splashing the bears. This angered the largest and she hit the surface with such force that the water erupted like a geyser. Now all three started roaring with rage. If the Game Department hadn't been 500 miles away I would have forthwith handed in my resignation as a Yukon outfitter at that moment.

It had all started the previous winter when I asked my husband, Louis: "Is it all right with you if I apply for a big game outfitter's license and have the area around Lancing and Ortell lakes?"

I had been toying with the idea some time. I had great admiration for Belle Desrosier, of Whitehorse, daughter of a retired Mounted Policeman. She was beautiful, an outstanding hunter, a crack shot, and best of all, she was a Yukon outfitter. It sort of irked me that she was of such tremendous help to Curly, her husband, while I had only been cooking beans for Louis, my outfitter husband.

Louis's reply seemed somewhat exaggerated. "Sure, sure, good idea, go right ahead."

I wouldn't have been so thrilled over his consent had I known it was given because he was so sure the Game Department would turn me down.

When the official document arrived proclaiming me a full-fledged Yukon Big Game Outfitter, we were both stunned. It suddenly hit me full force that I was lacking in some very necessary qualifications which the Game Department assumed I had. Consequently, I boned up fast on how to be a good outfitter — especially on how to tie diamond hitches, how to read maps, and how to manage a staff of Indian guides who consumed enough rum to keep the Yukon at the top of Canadian alcohol consumption statistics.

For the first time, Louis helped with the bookings and I noticed we booked more women than usual. He turned thumbs down on my hunting in my area, so far from where he would be hunting. Instead, he lent me part of his area on the Bonnet Plume River. He would be hunting about fifty miles below me. He also gave me his gentlest horses, and guides who had acquitted themselves more on their ability to hunt than in their capability of getting into trouble.

Both of our parties camped three miles below Fairchild Lake, on the Bonnet Plume River. I was waiting for my hunters to come by plane, and sent Alec to pack them down. Louis's party was ready to leave. My head buzzed with my husband's instructions. Louis took a long time to kiss me goodbye, as if it might be the last time. "Remember, your rifle is a helluva lot more important than your lipstick," was his parting advice.

The guides watched Louis depart, looking like a pack of mournful hounds ordered to stay home from a coon hunt. To cheer them, I mentioned that a woman would be one of the next hunters. They perked up.

"Mrs. Brown, is she young?"

"No doubt."

"Is she pretty?"

"Probably."

Before I knew it, I had a mutiny on my hands. Each man claimed that his qualifications justified his being selected as her guide.

My suggestion to draw straws was scornfully ignored. Their suggestion to fight it out, and may the best man win, sent me into panic.

Alec was due to arrive with the hunters any minute. If any of my crew was knocked out or crippled, I knew that Alec would hightail it down the Bonnet Plume River to Louis. Louis had hinted that he would be expecting a messenger with a plea to come bail me out of some disaster.

At the sound of shod hoofs striking rocks, the guides forgot about fighting and craned their necks to get the first glimpse of the female hunter. Suddenly I thought of a solution and turned to talk again to the guides, but there wasn't an Indian in sight. So swiftly had they vanished, I had been unaware of their leaving.

A few moments later I had proof that my Indian guides' boasts of 20-20 vision were true. Following Alec was a woman who extended amply on both sides of the saddle. Her stiff and short grey hair stuck out from under a stocking cap, and smoke wreathed her head from a pipe she was puffing.

I breathed a sigh of relief. The mutiny was over. Later I found the mutiny was still on, but in reverse.

The woman could have drunk my Finnish brother-in-law under the table. The astonishing amount of booze she consumed almost shortened this outfitter's career. It certainly shortened my hair.

In the evenings, the hunters liked to have their coffee and dessert served around the campfire. One late afternoon I made a plum pudding, soaked sugar cubes in brandy to circle the lush treat, then carried it to the campfire for the grand finale. Harry McGinty, one of the guides, lit match after match, but the pudding wouldn't take fire. Disgusted, our female imbiber snorted, "Wait," and stalked to her tent.

102

She returned with a bottle of clear alcoholic liquor and dumped its contents over the pudding. Before I could set it down, Harry stuck a lighted match over the pudding. WOOSH ... off went my eyebrows, eyelashes, and bangs!

The hunters brought in game, all right, but not the quality to win me the brand new Ski-Doo that Louis and I had bet for the outfitter bringing in the largest trophy.

I had two more hunts scheduled, but this wasn't a good start. Then, bless her dear old heart, our hefty imbiber brought in a moose rack that, when stood on end, towered over my head. I could have kissed her. I was sure that none of Louis' hunters would equal it. The old girl proved such a good sport and such a crack shot that I almost cried when she left.

In the next party was a Women's Libber. I was neither for nor against Women's Libbers. I knew nothing about them. It was most unfortunate that the first night around the campfire she took it upon herself to make sure we knew and understood the platform of Women's Liberation. As she heatedly expostulated on the inadequacy of men compared to women, I glanced at the guides and froze. Their stolid, blank expressions and narrowed eyes didn't fool me a bit. I knew there was trouble brewing. I hardly slept that night, trying to figure out in advance how to block any measures the guides might take. Late the next afternoon I knew I was too late.

I had just put on a fresh pot of coffee when I was startled at the apparition that appeared between the tent flaps. Dripping with mud and ooze, the Libber staggered in and slumped on a pack box. She was closely followed by guide Lonny Johnny. I never saw a more innocent looking Indian. But I knew he was as guilty as Satan when he said: "Mrs. Brown, man had to save her. Dumb woman, get stuck in mud."

When she tried to explain, I knew she hadn't the faintest idea that the shrewd scheming of her guide had got her into the mess. I had the idea of guiding her myself the next day, but had to give it up when one of the guides brought in an injured horse.

But before Lonny started out with her again, I took him into the cook tent and glared at him. "Lonny, I want you to bring back your hunter INTACT. "

"What intact?"

"SAFE, SECURE, UNHURT, UNINJURED, UNHARMED, UNEXPOSED TO DANGER, AND BROUGHT BACK INTACT. SAVVY?"

"Sure, sure, Mrs. Brown, I savvy. But she smart woman. Know everything," Lonny's mouth curled bitterly.

"LONNY?"

"Sure," and Lonny stalked out, a dignified picture of injured masculinity.

About two o'clock that afternoon when I heard feminine sobbing, I was ready to scalp one Indian. However, when Lonny came into the cook tent, partly dragging his hunter, his face was four shades lighter than his usual swarthiness, and he looked so scared, I was sure that whatever had happened, he wasn't at fault.

The lady had fallen off her horse, and her foot had caught in the stirrup. She was lying on the ground, kicking and yelling.

Lonny explained to me: "I tell her, `shut up, you scare horse.'"

Being some distance in front of her, Lonny had unsheathed his rifle and was ready to shoot the horse if it bolted. He finally reached her, but it was impossible to get her foot loose because she had a large foot in an odd-shaped boot. Lonny could think of only one thing to do, and how he did it I'll never know. It would take a lot of rocks in his pockets to make him weigh 135 pounds. The lady was large and rawboned, and weighed at least 175 pounds. The horse was more than 16 hands tall. But that little Indian had somehow managed to get her back into the saddle and her foot out of the stirrup. All she had to show for the mishap was a badly twisted and swollen ankle.

Lonny, of course, made sure his hunter understood it was a man who had rescued her from the predicament she had brought upon herself.

I felt it would have been a disgrace to me as an outfitter if one of my hunters failed to bag at least one of the big four — a moose, a caribou, a sheep, or a grizzly. Knowing the Women's Libber to be a poor shot, I was delighted to see Lonny leading his horse in with antlers strapped to the saddle, but I was unprepared for the little Indian's fury. He was almost dancing up and down with rage when he reported to me.

"She shoot Santa Claus' reindeer. "

"WHAT?"

"I tell her not to shoot that one. I tell her to shoot other one."

Sure enough, Lonny was right. She had shot a castrated reindeer, probably strayed from the government herd at East Channel, McKenzie.

Lonny's eyes blazed: "Tell her, sure as hell, Mounted Policeman goin' arrest her."

I couldn't have been happier or more relieved when I saw her off on a plane, heading back for a Women's Lib convention somewhere or other.

As one bush plane departed, another arrived bringing new hunters. When I saw the difficulty the pilot had unloading one passenger, I grew alarmed. Surely there was some mistake. The man leaned heavily on a cane. The hunter I had corresponded with had impressed me as being at least a potential challenger for the heavyweight boxing championship.

I shook his hand with some trepidation. "You can't be ... ?"

"Why can't I be?" his old eyes were twinkling. "I knew if I told you I was over eighty you wouldn't take me."

"But you said ... "

"Hell yes. I said a lot. Wanted one more hunt before I kick the bucket. Had three heart attacks already."

I tried to flag down the departing plane, but it was too late, and I was left with a potential corpse. Even seeing a bear might frighten him into oblivion, I thought.

At camp, his contagious humor was unsurpassable. He kept us roaring with laughter. He had been a sergeant in the horse marines in China. The guides were kept in speechless awe as he narrated hair-raising tales of his exploits in China. The old guy couldn't walk, but my, how he could ride! The guides took him to a mountain where rams were feeding on high ridges. He made a miraculous shot and got his ram. Every hunter until doom's day will hear about it from those guides.

His arthritis bothered him, so he decided to cut short his hunt, but the old horse marine was happy; his last hunt had given him a Dall ram. When we parted, we were both fighting to keep back the tears.

We pulled out with the last hunting party of the season, heading for the place I mentioned first, and there I met my greatest challenge. Across the stream a sloping mountain was afire with autumn's red, orange and yellows, making a wild and beautiful backdrop for the three silvertips. Their shadows reflected, dark and ominous, in the water, mirroring an opal-pink sunset. But there was no time for scenery appreciation. I knew my next move would be crucial for both the grizzlies and me. Had there been a tree tall enough, I would have climbed it. Just then Alec, having heard my shot, came running.

"Get your gun," I yelled.

Again the grizzlies started wading toward me. I put another shot in front of them. This time they stopped and raised up on hind legs. This was unnerving, as grizzlies sometimes charge from a standing position. They looked huge.

Alec returned, on the run and out of breath. Kneeling together, we both fired as close as we dared without hitting them. The grizzlies hit the water and started toward us. This time Alec and I fired twice in rapid succession. The grizzlies backed out of the stream and walked along the shore. We watched anxiously, as they slowly circled. But they weren't leaving.

It was growing dark. Alec built a large campfire, and tied the horses closer to the tents. We sat by the fire with our rifles across our knees. Now and then a horse screamed and broke loose, plunging through the brush in terror. When all was still again and we heard the crackling of brush, we knew the grizzlies were still narrowing their circle. Sometimes we heard a low growling.

That night was seven years long and I had plenty of time to think. Bitterly I realized that the select finishing school for girls in Walla Walla, Washington had neglected to develop in me the stamina, guts and resourcefulness it takes to make a successful outfitter. I'd happily have gone back to cooking beans under Louis' protection.

When another horse screamed and broke loose, my nerves were about ready to explode. Grabbing a blazing branch, I flung it out into the darkness. It landed in a patch of dead spruce. In seconds it was a blazing inferno.

Alec and I didn't feel safe in leaving our campfire until a beautiful pink tinted sunrise gave us courage.

We found no trace of the three grizzlies.

At home I counted three grey hairs. I named then Grizzly Number One, Grizzly Number Two, and Grizzly Number Three.

If I had admiration and respect for Belle Desrosier before my stint at outfitting, afterward it was multiplied a million times. Belle is still outfitting, and the Yukon government — and all Women's Libbers — can be proud of her success.

But I won a consolation prize — a brand new Ski-Doo Nordic.

Chapter 13

HOT DOGS ON ICE

The Far North is redundant with galvanizing and hazardous tales of loveable and cussable huskies. History records legendary feats of their courage and stamina. Admiral Byrd called them the infantry of his Polar explorations while others have dubbed them the saviors of the North.

However, at this particular moment, Norman Neddery was calling them something else. "YOU - SONS - OF - A - BITCHES - WHOA!"

Norman, a long time fur trapper in the Yukon, was returning from checking his trapline in the Mt. Ortel area. The day was warm for a Northern March, the toboggan was heavy with martin, lynx and fox furs. The ice on the Stewart River gave no traction and the pulling was hard on the huskies. Norman decided to give the team a rest before climbing up the steep bank to his cabin. They lay on the ice gulping snow, cooling off. Norman tightened a loose moose babish on his load and took a chew of snoose. A crash of splintering wood made the huskies leap to their feet and Norman sprang on the toboggan yelling "MUSH"!

Topping the riverbank, the huskies sniffed the air with alert interest. Another shattering of wood jerked Norman's head around. Cursing at what he saw, he flipped the toboggan over to anchor and standing on the traces, he jerked his 30-30 from its moose skin scabbard, carefully taking aim. The huskies, spotting the grizzly ripping open the wooden planked door to the log cache, took off in hot pursuit, throwing Norman on his back. The gun fired into the air and Norman lay sputtering and spitting snoose. Entangled in the traces, he desperately thrashed around, trying to take aim, while the huskies slid him on the seat of his pants, straight for the grizzly. Norman kept yelling "STOP-YOU-SON-OF-A-BITCHES-STOP!", with full intentions of shooting the huskies instead of the bear.

The old trapper cussed himself for being such a sap-headed fool. The big boar had been hanging around for weeks, even eating out of the dog dishes. Norman liked having him around because he was such a beautiful silver tip specimen. It sort of helped with the loneliness and kept the pesky black bears away. On a couple of occasions, Norman had seen grizzlies kill black bears, so they had good reason to stay away.

The toboggan slammed against one of the cache's supporting posts and hung up on a protruding limb. Thwarted in their pursuit, the huskies howled in protest, snarling and jumping, trying to climb the notched log ladder to the fifteen foot high platform. The grizzly, having eaten several meals with them, paid no attention and kept tugging the quarter of moose meat from the cache's small supply cabin on top.

The huskies, furious over their immobility, began fighting among themselves. Before Norman could untangle himself, the bear leaped to the ground with his meal and made off into the brush. Norman, with an injured leg, could only hobble to his cabin.

That night Norman pondered his problem. The grizzly, having started emptying the cache, wouldn't stop until he'd transported all of the winter-killed moose to where he'd bury it. He would then lie on top guarding it and woe to any man or beast who came near.

Living for forty years over a hundred miles from his nearest neighbor on a remote trapline with his Indian wife, Sanoa, Norman could pay heavily for a small mistake. He had failed to cut down a large lightening-killed tree and it had fallen sloping against the cache. The grizzly easily walked up the log and jumped onto the platform.

Once the meat was gone, the bear could get ugly. He might even start killing the huskies. It had happened to Joe Black's team. Starvation was not unknown in the Far North and the meat was all he, Sanoa and the dogs had to eat until he sold his furs. The Yukon is well known for its extremes in temperatures, and if there was a sudden weather change, sending the thermometer to below the fifties, it could be hell going the hundred miles on an empty stomach. There was only one thing to do and he'd rather jump into the frigid water of Lansing Creek than to do it.

Early the next morning he unsnapped the chain on his leader's collar. Tip kept order in the team and was full of fight. Norman followed the grizzly's track up the trail. When the tracks faded into the underbrush, Norman gave the command Tip had eagerly been waiting for. He disappeared around the bend at full speed, only to reappear racing in full retreat with the grizzly gaining on his plumed tail. Norman stepped behind a tree and, as they passed, felled the silver tip with one shot. Tip, regaining his courage, grabbed the fallen bear by the throat, growling savagely. Norman sadly shook his head. "Why in God's name didn't you mind your own business, so we could live in peace with each other?"

Wherever there are huskies, there is always action and, more often than not, the unexpected. Jay Jackson, who's trapping territory was over on LaSell Creek, decided to pay a visit to his friends over at Loon Lake, a few miles away. He started out with a full team of eight huskies hauling a toboggan carrying a gift of a quarter of moose meat. Reaching the lake, he signaled his leader to GEE and follow the two-mile trail around the lake. Just then his friends' two hounds caught their scent and began vocalizing a warning of an approaching invasion. Jay's team took this as a challenge. In spite of Jay's shouts of "Gee", and the leader's effort to stay on the broken trail around the lake, the team took a short cut straight across the lake. Twenty feet out from solid shore ice, the toboggan broke through, sinking Jay ankle deep in the frigid waters of the lake. The huskies, ignoring what was happening behind, kept up the momentum, galloping fast enough to turn the toboggan into a surfboard. Blinded by the flying spray and soaked to the skin, Jay's only hope was to keep the huskies to their original intention. If the team slowed down, the toboggan would sink, dragging him and the dogs into the frigid depths.

His friends, hearing the loud vocalization, rushed for their binoculars and by the time Jay arrived, crusted in ice, they were bursting with hysterical laughter.

Danger always lurks on the trappers' trails, and the Northern huskies are vulnerable to wolf attacks, grizzly maulings, moose encounters, tough trails, and weather conditions.

A husky team belonging to Al Peterson had a harrowing experience with a wolf attack over at Elliot Lake. While trapping for wolverine, Al had the bad luck of catching his arm in a 330 conibear trap. The trap was clenched so tightly on the sleeve of his parka he couldn't free himself. It was over a hundred miles to help and he doubted he could stand the pain for that long. A pack of wolves could be heard coming up the valley and if they smelled the blood trickling over his hand, he was in for trouble. He jerked loose a piece of rope dangling on the toboggan. Tying one end tightly to the cuff of his parka and the other end around an arctic spruce, he tried sliding the trap down his arm, by pulling the end rope wrapped around the tree. The trap seemed to dig deeper into his arm.

In desperation he forced his arm muscles to relax and steadily pulled. Inch by inch the trap moved down his arm. With a firm jerk, it was off, leaving him weak with relief. His arm and hand were numb. Painfully flexing his fingers, he strove to bring back the circulation.

Straightening the team in their harness, he started back to his base cabin. He was travelling through a thick stand of Arctic spruce when, without warning, the wolf pack attacked the team. His gun wrapped in a frozen moose hide on the sled made it almost impossible to unsheathe with the tangle of fighting wolves and dogs jerking the toboggan around. Snatching the skinning knife from his belt, he frantically slashed at the frozen skin. Clawing out his gun, his first shot went wild because he could not hold steady with only one arm and hand. Three of his huskies were already dead. Slamming his rifle against his hip, he fired. Not until he emptied the chamber did the wolves give up. Al had killed two of them. With yammering howls, the rest of the wolves took off up an alluvial fan at the mouth of Links Pass. With the remains of his crippled team Al headed for his cabin, grateful for having survived.

The lure of the chase inherited from their wolf ancestors makes even the best trained husky hard to control in big game country. Once my husband, Louis, was trapping over on the Bonnet Plume River and lost his whole team during a large caribou migration. He was travelling down the river when a herd of migrating caribou unexpectedly broke out of a side canyon. In spite of his commands, the team lunged off in hot pursuit. Louis jumped on the brake with such force it snapped the traces. Free of the toboggan, the dogs raced out of sight, followed by a pack of wolves that had been trailing the caribou. For three days Louis waited for the return of his team, but by the tone of the wolves, he was sure they had fallen prey to the marauding predators. He had close to 90 miles to walk back to the small frontier town of Mayo.

Zitzie, our largest husky, could testify to the accuracy of a statement made by one of Barnum and Bailey's veterinarians, who believed the grizzlies had more strength in their forearms than any other animal he treated, and was therefore the most dangerous.

We were camped at Carpenter Lake, where the many colonies of Arctic Marmots inhabiting the low pass attracted a large population of grizzly. I was alone in the hunting camp with Zitzie and I knew a grizzly was around because all the caribou and moose meat had been dragged down from the tree cache. Although grizzly tracks were all over camp, Zitzie had given no warning. The nights were getting dark, so before dusk I decided to climb to the safety of our high cache. No sooner had I gained the platform than a white collared grizzly came rushing up the trail. Zitzie, deciding he better do some protecting, attacked the bear's rear. The grizzly swung around and with one swoop tossed Zitzie's hundred and twenty pounds over a twelve foot high clump of willows as if he were a baseball.

Dennis Heasley, the Yukon Government's regional supervisor of Social Services in Mayo, came from the Eastern Arctic, where he had his own close brushes with bears when driving his team of Siberian huskies out on the tundra from Churchill. There, the Chippewyan commands were most used for the teams. "Huw", meaning go right, "Cha" to go left, "Marche" meaning walk (but corrupted to "mush"). Dennis has reasons to remember the intense whiteouts, when the leader was hardly visible. He admitted it was scary at times and with good reason. Once, when hunting caribou and everything had a misty, vivacious vagueness, a large ghost like apparition passed in front of Rambler, his leader. Luckily, the polar bear kept travelling, for many are the Arctic tales of them taking on a dog team.

A closer call, in another whiteout, was when he drove over a polar bear. In the tundra there are deep depressions, and in one of these a bear was evidently having a nap. Dennis said he felt something soft underneath and looked down to see the sled was on top of a polar bear. The huskies needed no urging from Dennis to get out of there fast.

Dog teams are getting fewer and I was dismayed when word got to me that Dennis had sold all his huskies; then I was amused when he bought them all back. I ask him why? "Huskies are in my blood," he replied. Like the rest of us, he had one husky nearest to his heart. Rambler was the leader, the dog that could be depended upon to keep the line tight when harnessing a ten to twelve-dog team. Dennis said he could never manage that many huskies without him. Rambler always knew when anyone fell off the sled and would wait. He was a genius in sniffing out treacherous over-flows and would swing the team around the thin ice covering them. Rambler worked hard and all he wanted was affection.

In the Arctic beautiful beaded and embroidered back pads were made for each member of the team and an eight to ten inch high projection from the collar in bright yarns of tassels and streamers were worn to show respect for the leader. The leader himself wore a more elaborate decoration. Now that the modern harness has replaced the old style donut collar, this custom is hard to maintain.

I have had only one husky attack me and, had his chain been one inch longer, he would have slit my jugular vein. Furious that my kindness had been rewarded with such hate, I picked up a board. When Taku regained consciousness, he wobbled as he got to his feet and offered his paw. We shook and after that, I couldn't come near him, but that his paw was extended to be shaken. We became the best of friends and I could always trust him.

Like Rambler, Zitzie was special. He too worked hard to gain affection but, most of all, he wanted attention, to be admired. Oh, how he schemed to get it. His big brown eyes had won the hearts of some guests who pleaded for him to be unchained. While we were visiting, I saw out of the corner of my eye Zitzie trotting back and forth. No one paid any attention. Soon there was some wild squawking. The big mutt got our attention, for we all dashed to him to rescue the chicken he was carefully carrying in his mouth.

After Alaska magazine published my article about Zitzie, many readers wrote inquiring about my favorite husky. There must be thousands of tales told about this wonderful Northern dog conquering insurmountable obstacles to open up the North. Famous Northerner Charles E. Gillham tells it best in his immortal poem Sled Dogs. I quote the last two verses of his eloquent tribute to the husky:

Most amazing was God's forethought,
How wondrous was his plan
Developing the Husky dog,
The ally and friend of man.
You on the creeks and the tundra
You in the squalid igloo
Give thanks to God for the Husky
Who gave the great North to you.

Chapter 14

THE SWISS CHOCOLATE GRIZZLY

"Shoot" whispered the guide, his voice crisp with tension as his eyes flicked over his hunter for a quick check.

Severango Menelli, looking through his telescopic sights, hesitated as a large, dark form emerged from the shadows. Lowering his rifle, he shook his head, "Nein, nein, nein. You play big joke on poor Swiss man."

"Shhh, I'm telling you, it's a bear."

Menelli took another quick look then gulped air. "Nein, too big. It's a horse."

"All right, if it's a horse where's its tail?" his guide asked in exasperation, hoping the big grizzly didn't tear the camp to pieces before he convinced his hunter. The trophy that Menelli had crossed an ocean to bag was now boldly heading for the tent where his three hunting companions were frantically digging a hole in order to bury a box of Swiss chocolates a fun-loving cook had warned was a grizzly's favorite food.

The hunt had started 12 days previously in Yukon's scenic Bonnet Plume country, where Menelli, Fritz Lanz, Herter Rene and Armando Corti, all from Switzerland, landed at Fairchild Lake to be met by their outfitter and my husband, Louis Brown, with his staff of Indian guides.

Lanz had hunted with Louis before, and when he made the introductions, a wicked gleam came into his eyes. "And this is eight shot Menelli," he said.

Menelli threw up his arms in protest. "Nein, nein, one shot. I get my bear in one shot. You wait. You see."

"One-shot Menelli," someone shouted, and all joined in the laughter. The guides, Doc Johnny, Harry Baum, and Johnson Edward, grinned from ear to ear. They had guided Swiss before. They knew this was going to be a good hunt. These men put appreciation and enjoyment of the wilderness and wildlife first, and gave full credit to their guides for their skill in tracking, stalking and knowing the nature and habits of wild game.

While darkness blotted the lengthening shadows, and gauzy northern lights searched among the stars, Frenchy, the cook, took a blackened pot from glowing coals, sending showers of sparks sifting upward through dark branches of arctic spruce. Pouring strong, hot coffee, Frenchy chided the hunters. "You fellows came a helluva long ways to see more mountains. Stacked up against your Alps, our Bonnet Plume Mountains must look like ant hills."

Lanz shifted away from drifting smoke. "Ah, my friend, we came to breathe."

Next day, the party started leisurely hunting down the Bonnet Plume River. Reaching the mouth of Rapitan Creek, Louis sent the party up the valley for sheep and bear while he remained to supervise establishment of base camp.

Two days later the party returned. Rene and Lanz each bagged a grizzly, leaving Corti and, especially, Menelli the butt of much ribbing.

That evening Frenchy served crisp, golden brown sheep ribs roasted over glowing campfire coals, with scalloped corn and green bean salad, but he grumbled and growled when he had to stir up a second batch of mashed potatoes. However, when Lanz praised his blueberry pie, Frenchy quickly regained his good humor, beaming broadly as he served second helpings.

Upriver the grunting of a moose was drowned by shouts of laughter and whoops of merriment. The Swiss were having a lively game of cards in their tent.

Harry and Frenchy couldn't resist having a look. When Corti saw two pairs of curious eyes he waved them in, shoving a large box of Swiss chocolates at them. Frenchy recoiled with a well feigned look of horror. "My God. y-y-you brought chocolate into grizzly country?"

The merriment suddenly ceased as all eyes turned to Frenchy. Menelli said. "We bring big treat from Zurich. What wrong?"

"WRONG?" Frenchy clutched his hair. "A grizzly will walk miles, tear down caches, rip tents to get chocolate!"

Harry, trying to swallow his glee, doubled up in a spasm of coughing. Frenchy, well aware of the cause, yelled at him. "Scatter your germs outside! Get out of here."

Menelli watched the departure of his guide with concern. "Perhaps have flu?" he asked.

"Naw," drawled Frenchy, "Harry knows grizzly from A to Z and when he saw the chocolate he was so scared it choked him."

Lanz shoved three boxes of chocolate at Frenchy. "For you, my friend."

"Friend?" Frenchy snorted in derision. "Enemy, I'm afraid. My hide is too precious to accept."

Lanz gave a half-hearted laugh. "Now, Frenchy, you..."

"Right now a grizzly is making fast tracks for your chocolate," said Frenchy, and then quickly dived out of the tent.

The four Swiss argued hotly whether Frenchy was playing another joke on them. Menelli finally settled the matter by declaring, "Grizzly in camp? Nein, nein, too many man smells."

The Swiss played a boisterous game of cards until midnight. After silence crept over camp, a lone wolf on a distant ridge gave voice to the solitude.

Suddenly, Louis was awakened from a sound sleep. Raising on his elbow, he listened intently. Years spent alone in this remote, uninhabited wilderness had schooled him to the necessity of alertness. He was sure some danger had awakened him. He shut his eyes, concentrating to catch the slightest sound. Then he heard it — a faint clink, a heavy tread. Now he caught rank odor.

Bear! The wall of the tent gave a slight ripple. The bear was too close to risk startling him. Louis cursed himself for leaving his gun hanging on a tree near the dying campfire. Picking up two skinning knives, he lightly tapped them together to let the bear know the tent was occupied. The stillness was oppressive. Then the heavy treading passed the tent and Louis let out a breath of relief.

Peering through the tent flap he saw the grizzly standing, his silver tipped fur shimmering in the moonlight. For a moment, the big bear paused in front of the hunters' tent. Louis grinned to himself, wondering what the reaction of the two unsuccessful bear hunters would be if at that moment they decided to step out of their tent.

After watching the grizzly leave the clearing, Louis quickly retrieved his gun and put it at the head of his sleeping bag, in case the bear returned in a less pleasant mood.

At breakfast, Menelli accused Frenchy: "You try to put big scare on — what you say? — cheechako."

Frenchy assumed an air of injured innocence, but the tables were

115

turned on him the next moment when Louis led them outside to show the grizzly tracks in the sandy trail.

There was a stunned silence. Then the Swiss, pointing excitedly, broke into loud laughter. Rene patted Louis on the shoulder. "You and Frenchy big jokers. You help that clever cook to put one big scare over on us, but we figure you out. Last night you take Fritz's bear hide, you take his paw. You make tracks. We on to your big joke." The Swiss roared with laughter but Frenchy, looking at the grizzly tracks not two feet from the head of his bed, swallowed his snuff.

"Honest, I'm telling you the truth," Louis tried to assure them, "those tracks were made by a real grizzly and I'm sure he'll be back tonight."

"How you sure?" Corti asked with suspicion.

"Because from my years of hunting experience I know the habits of grizzly," answered Louis.

They were still unconvinced, but they teased Menelli: "Tonight you shoot the bear."

"Sure, sure, I get him one shot," laughed Menelli.

When they were leaving for the day's hunt, Louis told them. "You fellows be back early. I want you to have your supper by 6pm and everyone quiet in their tent."

During the day, Louis and Jimmy Davis, the wrangler, built a cache about six feet high. Jimmy was always nervous around bears and thought it should be at least four feet higher. They built a rifle rest, Louis wanting to make sure the grizzly wouldn't merely be wounded so close to the tents.

After supper, Corti, Lanz, and Rene kidded Menelli about his bear. They still thought it a big joke. Louis went over to their tent, trying to quiet them. They told him, "you mighty fine actor, but we not dumb."

Finally, Louis was able to procure a promise from them to be quiet for half an hour. Soon after 6pm, he looked out over the horse pasture, about 50 yards from camp where he kept the salt blocks, and saw the grizzly swinging down the horse trail. The bear was striding along as if he knew this was his domain and had no fear of man or beast.

Louis went swiftly over to the hunters' tent. "Where's Menelli?" he asked.

Rene shrugged. "He go to see what bees in Frenchy's bonnet now."

Louis held back the tent flap. "Take a look at Menelli's grizzly."

They gave Louis an amused glance, then more or less to humor him, looked out. Suddenly it was deadly still. Wide-eyed, they looked at each other then tiptoed to take another peek.

Louis grabbed Menelli's gun and ran to the cook's tent. With one look at his boss' set face, Frenchy hurriedly steered Menelli to the cache, growling low, "You better get him in one shot or there'll be a helluva mess."

While Louis watched the grizzly, Menelli, with fumbling fingers, was trying to replace his telescopic sights. This custom of the Swiss to carry rifle and telescopic sights separately until game was spotted almost drove Louis wild.

The grizzly sniffed the salt block, then walked to the guides' tent where some dried meat and fat hung on a ridgepole. The weather was warm and the guides hadn't bothered to set up a stove. Harry stuck his head out through the stovepipe hole for a look. The grizzly, only six feet from him, looked up, watching. The wind blew Harry's hair on end, giving him a scared look, but Harry never moved a muscle.

The bear moved on, stopping in front of the tent flaps. Jimmy grabbed his rifle, shoving a shell into the chamber. "Me shoot him" he said.

Johnson lunged for the rifle. "No! Too close!" he whispered fiercely.

Jimmy, scared out of his wits, tried to jerk the rifle out of Johnson's hand, but Johnson stubbornly hung on. "Too close. You shoot him now, he kill us all."

All this whispering inside the guides' tent was not to the grizzly's liking and he started toward the Swiss tent.

Louis stiffened, wondering what in hell was going on in their tent, from which issued sounds like someone breaking rocks.

Now the grizzly moved into a clear place and Louis hissed: "Shoot!"

That was when Menelli balked, thinking the bear to be a horse.

Frenchy breathed heavily. "My God, you can't be that dumb."

Louis was surprised to see the gun weaving on the rail. Menelli, after full realization, couldn't seem to keep the sights on the grizzly.

The bear stalked out of sight behind one of the tents. Louis took Menelli by the arm, shifting him to the other rail so Menelli would be in position when the bear came out from behind the tent.

Seconds later the bear appeared, lumbering toward the cook tent. Frenchy swore under his breath, groaning: "He's heading for the pies."

Louis was now whispering so loudly trying to get Menelli to shoot that the bear heard them, turned and started back up the trail. He would soon be out of sight behind the tents. In desperation, Louis yelled, "SHOOT!"

Menelli fired one shot. The grizzly disappeared but they heard a faint grunt, then they could see the bear heading for a point of timber but still walking in his rolling gait. When he reached the timber Menelli took another shot, claiming, "I got him that time."

"Hell, that was a clean miss," Louis told him.

The grizzly disappeared in the timber and Louis climbed down from the cache to follow the tracks a short way. He soon returned, saying, "We'll have to hunt him again in the morning."

Then they entered the Swiss tent and Louis demanded to know what was going on in there earlier.

"Ssshhhh," they whispered. "We bury the chocolates. We want no bear here."

To their consternation, Louis sat down and laughed until tears ran down his cheeks.

Early the next morning, before anyone was up, Louis set out on the trail of the grizzly. A short distance away, in thick timber, he found the grizzly dead. The first shot had killed him.

As soon as Menelli finished his breakfast, Louis led him up the trail saying: "We'd better go and have a look for your bear."

Louis maneuvered Menelli in front of him when they drew close, Menelli saw the bear, and he stood

"Menelli, you sure lived up to your word. You killed him with one shot," said Louis.

Menelli was beside himself with joy. He yelled to his comrades: "I shoot him! One shot like I say."

Frenchy snorted: "Damn good thing or he'd busted this camp wide open."

The others came running and there was much backslapping and congratulations. But one thing puzzled them deeply. Clamping Frenchy on the shoulder, Corti asked, "how you know this grizzly smelling the chocolates?"

Chapter 15

STOP THE STAMPEDE

My husband, Louis, and I were waiting at Fairchild Lake, on the Bonnet Plume River in central Yukon, for the arrival of our two big game hunters; Jack Beban, a well known lumberman from Vancouver Island, and Rudy Pop, an energetic Austrian and popular furrier from the city of Vancouver.

Rudy wanted to film a caribou stampede for a Walt Disney club, of which he was a member. To catch the action, he had brought along a photographer's uninhibited selection of camera equipment. He should have brought along Yakima Kunut, choreographer for the chariot race in Ben Hur. Yakima could handle the caribou, but could he handle Rudy?

Jack wanted a caribou with double shovels. In one of his letters, he hinted to being a gourmet cook of oriental cuisine. He would also bring the makings for a salad. After two months on the trophy trails, I was starved for some greens and now I anxiously waited for the expected head of lettuce.

After waiting for several hours, we wondered how good Jack's navigating skills were, since he was piloting his own Beaver floatplane. When finally a sliver of silver glistened over the horizon, we cheered with relief.

Circling camp, after giving a couple of wing salutes, Jack made a perfect landing. Jovial greetings were exchanged, making the guides grin from ear to ear. They liked fun loving hunters who were quick on the quip.

Everyone pitched in to unload the plane. Crate after crate of lettuce, celery, tomatoes, cucumbers and avocados were tossed to shore, followed by cases of shrimp, crab, imported cheeses and specialties from India. When Jack presented me with a bouquet of radishes and parsley, I realized his idea of what it took to make a salad was the quintessential foresight of a chef d'oeuvre and I was scared to death to cook for him. Later, after he transformed a few simple ingredients into a sumptuous Chinese dish, I dubbed him Maitre Cusinier de Yukon.

It didn't take a head of lettuce or a can of shrimps to convince me this hunt wasn't going to be ordinary. How could it be when we were camped practically on a remote glacier, more than four hundred miles from the nearest super-market and would be eating twenty-five different kinds of salad, when we should be toughing it out on moose, caribou and Dall sheep meat?

My salad garnishes of radish roses impressed Jack, but failed to please the guides. Lonny Johnny disdainfully proclaimed: " No damn rabbit me. Want'm roast caribou ribs."

"Shovel it down" Louis replied, " We can't move until we eat this damn stuff up."

The trouble was, the caribou had migrated further East and we would have to fly to Palmer Lake to catch up with the herd, leaving our staff of guides and wranglers to bring the pack train to the high country, a three-day trip.

When I flatly refused to leave all the green produce, Louis argued, "It will all wilt if the pack train carry's it"

Jack tersely commented: "My Beaver isn't a cargo ship. We're overloaded now. Add a cabbage and we won't be able to get off the lake."

Rudy, wild to get started filming the caribou stampede, settled the matter "Bury the green garbage and let's get to the caribou."

We dug trenches just above permafrost and stored most of it, but my parka was bulging with all the salad makings I could stuff in my pockets unobserved.

Black cumulus clouds boiled over the mountains, whipping Fairchild into choppy waves. It took several tries before we cleared. Leaving the Bonnet Plume, we flew into the heart of the storm. Sleet hissed against the windows. Swirls of vapor shrouded us in an invisible world. Louis was trying to navigate without success. I was trying to forget the remembered jagged peaks in the area. Jack started singing snatches of popular song hits. If we crashed, at least he would be a cheerful corpse.

The wind buffeted us relentlessly and when we suddenly lost altitude, my stomach didn't follow. I vowed if I ever reached the blessed mother earth safely, I would here after stick to old Shorty's back for my transportation. Another burst of wind pushed fog away from a lopsided mountain and Louis had his bearings. "Hold to the right Jack, it isn't far."

When a curtain of scuttling clouds fled to the South, revealing the shimmering blue green waters of Palmer Lake nestled between powdered white glaciers, I felt I was descending to paradise.

Safely landed, Jack's first thought was food. "I'll cook a meal that will flip your tonsils" he jokingly bragged. Louis started pumping up the two burner gas stove, but Jack, spying one of our stored wood camp stoves, insisted: "Get some wood, I have to have the oven."

Louis started unpacking saws and axes. "There's a few trees up this gulch."

"None of that lumber jack stuff on my vacation," Jack snorted. "I want wood that's already cut."

Louis laughed: " Well, I know an old prospector with a wood pile in Mayo."

Jack ran for his plane: "Come on, let's buy the guy out."

Louis remonstrated: "Jack we have to start hunting. Sometimes a double shovel is hard to find."

Jack shouted over his shoulder: "If I don't get a double shovel this year, I'll get it next year."

Rudy and I watched the plane fly over camp, heading for Mayo, vowing it was the height of degradation to be roughing it in a big game camp and fly to town for fire wood.

Rudy started hanging cameras and film bags around my neck. My neck wasn't long enough so he started hanging camera accessories on my belt. He shouldered his AeroFlex camera and heavy tripod.

Two miles South of the lake we spotted about fifty caribou cows and calves crossing an alluvial fan dotted with yellow auriculas. Rudy started molting camera equipment, hesitated, and then decided. "No, takes hundreds to make a stampede. Where in hell are the big guys?"

We walked another mile, sitting down on a patch of caribou moss, to survey the surrounding alpine setting. Our 9 x 35 Bausch & Lomb binoculars picked up a small calf sound asleep on the edge of a deep ravine. We knew it wouldn't be alone so we crept closer, watching and waiting. When Rudy gave a loud gasp, I swung my glasses to where his were focused. The sun glistened on the tip of a polished horn. Slowly grazing to the top of the ravine, a big bull caribou stood in all his magnificent splendor. His snow-white cape fluffed around his large cinnamon shaded body. He stood testing the wind until given a shove from behind by three more bulls. Rudy whispered: "Double shovels!"

Shaking with nervous excitement Rudy prepared for filming. I was afraid the sound of the movie camera would spook them, but they paid no attention to us and after jerking up their heads and looking us over,

121

they resumed feeding. Now that his nap was over, the calf meandered over to give one of the bulls a playful shove. Rudy's face beamed with ecstasy.

Only when Rudy ran out of film did he stop. "Damn, I should shoot one of those bulls."

"Oh Rudy, you wouldn't do that, after they have posed so nicely for you."

Rudy hesitated, then whirled to watch a tiny speck in the sky growing larger. Overhead the Beaver dipped its wings. Rudy swore under his breath. "Looks like those damn fools stacked wood on the wings."

When Rudy and I arrived back in camp, the stove was cracking in the kitchen tent and a pile of chopped wood was being carried inside. Jack chortled "That's the way to get wood, let the other guy do the chopping." Turning to Rudy he snapped "Where's the horns?"

"Horns?" Rudy gave Jack a sheepish grin. "We sure shot caribou to-day, but not with guns. You see, the caribou had a guardian angel."

"With reddish hair?" Jack asked looking meaningful at me.

Rudy laughed "With blue eyes and..."

"CARIBOU, GET YOUR CAMERAS!!" Louis yelled excitedly.

A small herd of caribou was trotting down the South shore, while another herd on the opposite side was heading North. Among them were the large, white-caped bulls. Rudy clutched his iron-grey hair, shouting: "GET THEM INTO ACTION!"

"Don't be so damn particular!" Jack growled "Get click'n!"

Rudy excitedly snatched a brush and vigorously brushed at an offending speck of dust on his lens. A sudden gust of wind fluttered a canvas tarp, spooking both herds and by the time Rudy was back behind the camera there was only a barren shore to film.

It was growing late and we were very hungry when Jack disappeared into the kitchen tent, declining all offers of help. From within came merry whistling and gay snatches of song. If any one stuck their heads through the tent flaps, offering assistance, they were promptly shooed out.

One by one the stars twinkled in the darkening sky. The moon rose to top a snowy crested peak. The aurora borealis played over the jagged horizon as we kept looking longingly at the cook tent. None of us were brave enough to check on how the meal was progressing. When we were about to give up hope for relief for our rebellious stomachs, Jack popped his head yelling "come and get it you starved galoots!"

We rushed in. To say Jack's Chinese specialty was delicious would be an understatement. The flavors made a dream come true for the taste buds and happiness for the tummy. Only a master of the culinary art could have orchestrated such a gastronomical delicacy.

Two days later the pack train arrived. Lonny Johnny started a campfire to make tea and was startled when piling on more chopped wood, Louis yelled, "go easy on Hardrock MacDonald's wood pile."

"You crazy. Hardrock's in Mayo"

"Yea, but his wood pile's here"

Lonny shook his head muttering: "Fool white man, all time do things Indian not do."

Early the next morning, Lonny Johnny was sent out scouting to locate a large herd of caribou in a good location for filming, if possible. He came back to report. "Plenty caribou, not far"

"How many?" Louis queried.

"Oh maybe five hundred, maybe more, big lot."

"Where?"

"You know that place. Foots of glacier."

Louis turned to Rudy. "Sounds right for your stampede. Round up your camera gear and let's go. Lonny you…"

"Damn crazy white man! Why for he do that? Get him self damn killed! "

It wasn't until later that I fully appreciated Lonny's wisdom in refusing to have any part of the plan.

Jack spoke up. "Louis let Lonny go with me. Today I get a double shovel. Feel it in my bones."

"Ok, Lonny, you go with Jack and get him a caribou," Louis acquiesced.

Rudy, Louis and I set out to film the great Cecil B. Demille spectacular.

The valley was narrow and one end was black with caribou. While Rudy pondered on how to mastermind the action, Louis was testing the air currents and I was untangling myself from camera equipment.

Rudy was undecided as to the proper tactics, so we argued over our respective positions. Finally, Rudy decided he would set his cameras near the East end of the valley. Louis should station himself at the West end, start the stampede straight for the cameras. Across the valley to the South, towering peaks and glaciers would block any escape in that direction but there was an unimpeded sweep to the lake on the North. I was worried. "Rudy, what if they head straight for the lake?"

123

"You stop 'em" Rudy snapped, busy with his camera.

"ME? ME?"

"Wave your shirt and yell like hell," Rudy said shouldering his heavy tripod.

"Rudy, I can't stop them and..."

"Shoot over them. Louie when I give the signal, you start them so they'll come like banshee's on their tails."

Louis grinned. "Rudy, you better clean your lenses before I start them. They'll come fast."

"Louie, I don't want them poking. Let's get going before they smell your stinky shaving lotion."

I didn't like the all-alone feeling as I waited for Rudy's signal. A cow caribou uneasily stood up to look around. Two bulls warily got up to test the breeze.

They weren't the only ones who were nervous. I backed closer to a four foot boulder, wondering why Rudy wasn't giving the signal. I turned my binoculars on him. I couldn't tell what he was doing but he wasn't behind his camera. A dreadful thought flashed across my mind. At this crucial moment, was he dusting the lens?

A shout that wasn't from Louis echoed across the valley. The wrangler was bringing in a stray horse. The herd as one leaped up. Louis, thinking Rudy had given the signal he hadn't seen, began deflating his full lung capacity.

In full flight, the herd headed for the cameras. The valley seemed to vibrate under their flying hoofs. Suddenly Rudy started flailing both arms high in the air. Had some thing gone wrong? This sudden movement scared the caribou even more and, with a new burst of speed the whole herd leaned over circling.

Heading straight for the lake, the caribou hit the shale in a rumbling roar. Jagged horns blurred down on me. They didn't even notice I was in the way. I waved my red bandanna, tore off my shirt, furiously flapping it up and down screaming at the top of my lungs "STOP! STOP!"

This only made them gain speed. I could see their terror stricken eyes and I thought of Lonny Johnny and his keen Indian wisdom. Seeing I was going to be run over I leaped behind the boulder and made myself as small as possible. Brown legs swished past the boulder as a thundering roar filled my ears. Dust choked me.

Timidly peeking out, I saw an old, moth-eaten cow caribou forlornly limping behind. I knew just how she felt — deserted.

Back at camp, Jack was jubilant over his caribou, a real double shovel trophy. Rudy was strangely silent.

After the hunt we fully expected to hear the stampede had made a box office hit or even had won an Oscar, but Rudy never made mention of it again. Had Rudy finished the usual dusting of the lens when the caribou took off or hadn't he?

We never knew what really happened to that hot action, but one thing we do know, they were two of the finest sportsmen it's been our pleasure to guide.

Chapter 16

A HOLE IN THE YUKON

Today, everyone wants to be an expert. It doesn't matter what you are an expert on, just so you are an expert. I am an expert on outhouses. Thirty years experience with two holers.

When Chief Robert Hager, of the Na Cho Nyak Dun, Mayo Indian band, made a derogatory remark over the air waves about outhouses, I felt it my duty to remind the Chief that, not long ago, the only privacy his people had was behind bushes. A privy would have looked like the Royal Hilton.

The outhouse is the oldest architectural structure retaining its original functional design. The hole is always round.

In early France, the outhouse was known as 'pis de terre' because they were built of rammed earth. The Romans built this type of construction throughout conquered Europe. A Parisian told me France still has four hundred year old earth latrines. In Africa, it's known as the `long drop' and in the United State as the `necessary house' or 'privy'. The New York Times, updating the elimination etiquette in privacy, reveals any remaining privies are now transformed into tool sheds, pool cabanas, and play houses.

If any of these edifices remain intact South of the border, it must be in Texas, where antiques are highly cherished and jealously guarded. Knowing Texans, they would give the same reverence to an antiquated outhouse as a Frenchman would give to Versailles. But it's in the Northern wilderness of the Yukon where its popularity survives, comme il faut. The favorite construction being logs and gas cans.

Today one can well envy Yukon's early outhouse entrepreneurs. They built when no building permits were required, when there were no building inspectors, no architects, no construction costs and no taxes. Best of all, building sites were free and any plot that took the fancy of the builder went uncontested. Some of their choice of sites would send any architect into apoplexy and a paleontologist into dementia.

One such architectural gem is approximately fifty-five miles North East of Mayo, a place known as Maynard Creek. My husband was with a prospecting party when a member of the group visited a half-rotted derelict partly perched over a swift-moving creek. They discovered the swirling current was washing some very interesting and unusual bones from under the outhouse. Later, scientists identified them as having belonged to a suborder ophidian, the size being comparable to that of a boa constrictor. I have been told that not since the Cretaceous period of seventy eight million years ago had snakes been in the Yukon. If true, the age of the Na Cho Nyak Dun Indian legends would be incredible. One being of an Indian woman who never returned from visiting her rabbit snares. When found, she was wrapped in the coils of an enormous snake.

Other Yukon outhouse sites have been found on mammoth and prehistoric buffalo bones and some unidentified skulls. Not being a paleontologist, I could only marvel over the whole parade of prehistoric life found under privies.

Mt. Hilton rises six thousand, seven hundred and fifty five feet above the Lilliputian frontier settlement of Keno City. From this aggregation of rugged sourdoughs winds a rutted, rocky, narrow road, climbing up to a questionable altitude of rarefied air that is the home of the frosted Hoary Marmots. Far below, one can see the shimmering lakes of Hanson, McQuestion and Ladue. Beyond, is the vast Ogilvie Range, an uninhabited wilderness of unsurpassed beauty. The centerpiece of this magnificent panorama is an outhouse perched precariously over the edge of a tremendous precipice. This building site would make architect Karen Jacobson's face blanch, and she's the specialist in building roof top additions to the skyscrapers of New York City. To enter this alpine structure would be a breathless adventure in space.

An outhouse even played a part in the Russian revolution. Ed Barker, one of Yukon's gold dredge masters, was sent to Russia to instruct the Russians on how to mine gold. The dredging was a rich success, resulting in stockpiles of gold bricks, a percentage being Ed's pay. Just as Ed was congratulating himself on soon becoming a millionaire, the revolution erupted. As the Red army drew closer, Ed grew more worried. How could he escape with his gold bricks? Friendly Russians warned him it would be suicide to try and escape with his pay. Ed decided if he couldn't have the gold, neither could the Russians, but where could he hide it? In his frenzied extremity his eyes lit on the outhouse. Ahhh! The answer. Without delay, he dumped his gold bricks down the hole.

For over fifty years that Russian outhouse has been on Ed's mind.

Whenever he met my husband in town, he would start chuckling. "Hey, Louis, do you suppose those son-of-a-guns, ever found all that gold I chucked down the hole?"

"Ed, I doubt it."

"Well, I hope those SOBs are still digging for it."

Jessie and Don Carlston gave a unique twist to the outhouse as a symbol of enamoured love. Newly wedded, Jessie laughingly relates: " For our first Wedding anniversary, my better half built me a beautiful outhouse out of gas cans. How's that for an unusual gift to show devotion?"

Outhouses are even used to help celebrate the big day when gold was discovered in the Yukon. One of the highlights of Klondike Days is the Great Privy Race. Several privies on wheels pulled by teams of willing volunteers careen and jostle in merry competition as they race each other to the finish line.

It took the Yukon's Ellis Phillip to originate a keystone cop outhouse comedy. Ellis, a big Swede over six feet tall and pressing the scale down to two hundred and eight pounds, was working mining claims on McKay Hill with other miners when he stopped work to pay the outhouse a visit. He had just settled down when his companions yelled "Hey, Ellis, MOOSE, call him in so we can get a shot."

Ellis, renowned in the Yukon for his successful moose calling, obliged. From the outhouse came quivering, urgent call of a lovesick cow. Ellis then out did himself imitating a bull answering. There was an ominous crashing of brush. With blood shot eyes, roaring a fearful challenge, the slighted bull moose charged to do battle for his ladylove. The miners on their way to get their guns took to the trees instead. Ellis, not being able to see the outside action, kept bellowing. Suddenly, the outhouse disintegrated, sending kindling wood all over the landscape. With a yell, Ellis bolted out, only to bolt back in to the wreckage inches ahead of the massive spread of horns. One brave soul sprinted for his gun and stopped the action, but not before the moose had a piece of Ellis's pants on his horns.

If owning an outhouse has lowered our social status, it's immaterial and I'm not aware of it. Even if it did, it wouldn't matter because it's more important to be able to look every fish in the Stewart River in the eye and know I haven't polluted it. Yes, sad but true, one can no longer smell wild roses when near the Stewart River and I blame it on Queen Victoria. It was she who started the five-gallon flush. When Thomas Crapper installed the first automatic toilet in London's Royal Palace, it was Queen Victoria who first pulled the chain that started river pollution and her great- great grand daughter, Queen Elizabeth II, can't seem to stop it.

After snowshoeing to the outhouse all winter, fishing a wolverine out of the hole in the spring, arguing all summer with the hornets over the rights of occupancy, I started dreaming about outhouses, dreams which escalated into nightmares. One restless night, dreaming of desperately searching for a privy in zero temperatures, I was overjoyed to see in a grove of Arctic spruce a little red outhouse with a stove pipe belching smoke. Saved by a warm outhouse and the hole rimmed by a heating pad. What a relief.

"Hell, the roof's leaking" Louis yelled, waking me to the most embarrassing moment of my life.

At breakfast I told Louis: "You know the Yukon needs a motto."

"Like what?" Louis growled, forking another sourdough flapjack.

"What do you think of `Honi soit que mal y pense'?"

"What in hell does that mean?"

"Shamed be he who thinks evil of it."

"Of what?"

"Of Yukon outhouses."

"Of course no one should be ashamed of them. They gave the Vikings their endurance and fortitude."

"Great, now the Yukon outhouse has the same motto as England's Order of the Garter."

The great naturalists, such as John Muir, Enos Mills, or Edwin Teale, would have considered our outhouse an ideal spot from which to observe the wonders of nature. Through the doorless door, one has the unobstructed view of lakes, rivers, mountains and a whole parade of wildlife.

It's a shock to some of the visitors when they can't locate a door to our privy. Even when assured only a muskrat, moose or bear would peek, they still feel nervous.

A poet visiting from England went into raptures over the view. She was so overcome by the scenery seen through the doorless door, she wrote some of her best poetry while sitting on the observation hole watching the muskrats building their winter food cache in the lake below.

Olivia Sutherland, visiting us from Michigan, claimed our outhouse saved her life. My husband raised registered Scotch Highland cattle. Chieftain Roary, a pure bred bull, resented the smell of bears. A grizzly had been hanging around and every time Roary smelled his tracks he went into a rage. Olivia, seeing the bull break through the fence and lower his horns, fled to the closest building, the outhouse. Roary, spying the billowing sheets, attacked the clothesline. Finding little satisfaction there, he peered around and spotted the fluttering of skirts in the doorless door. With a great snort and bellowing roar, he charged the outhouse with such force it almost rocked the privy off the hole. Luckily for Olivia, his spread of horns was too wide to get through the door. Roary backed off for another try but Louis, hearing our guest screaming for help, came to the rescue.

Another visitor endeared herself by proclaiming: "I've just paid an interior designer a fabulous sum for designing the latest in lighting arrangement for my bathroom, but it simply can't compare with the Northern Light seen from your outhouse."

I can't remember just where I read about the story, but it was about a Queen who had an elegant and sumptuous Pagoda style privy. Rich tapestries hung on the wall and the perimeter of the hole was padded with brocade. Her royal guards always escorted with regal ceremony. Not until I read this account did I fully appreciate the honor bestowed on me by my own determined escort. If not royal, at least they were loyal. First Zitzie, an oversized husky, seeing the direction I take and shrewdly guessing my intention, heads the procession. MiMi, my silver grey poodle, daintily trots behind him, followed by Satan, a loveable black cocker spaniel. Not to be left out, Tommy Boy, a spoiled Yukon cat, races to head the procession, his plumed tail waving like a banner. If no squirrels are in sight, we traverse the twenty yards with dignified solemnity, but if Oscar the parka squirrel, guardian of our back yard, challenges us with insulting chatter, the procession breaks up into a yelping riot. This can be very disconcerting if there is haste.

Over the years, I've come up with a lot of theories for improving outhouse comfort, all of questionable value. I thought of a propane heating pad around the hole, but propane freezes at fifty below. A wood stove? Well, by the time one got an outhouse at eighty below zero warm enough to be comfortable, one would be out of the notion. The only thing I know to do is to call on all experts for a solution — and don't tell me to move to town and add to the river pollution. I'm proud that the Yukon still has in use many old outhouses. A reminder of a time when people had the proper respect for the rivers and streams, Mother Earth's life blood, and kept them pure and clean.

Chapter 17

HELL NO,
HE'S YOUR GUIDE

"THERE, MY BOSS, TOUGH BOSS HER," shouted a voice in broken English, with an undertone of laughter. Everyone in Danny's general delivery store turned to follow the brown finger pointing directly at me. Lonny Johnny, a small and wiry Indian, was highly amused over my embarrassment. He loved to tease and uproariously announced: "She save this Indian from big bear. She shoot'm damn good."

"Lonny, please stop" I begged. We looked at each other and it seemed we lived in that fleeting moment all the hardships, dangers, and fun we had shared on the big game trails of the Yukon.

"Sure boss," Lonny Johnny grinned, swaggering out the door. His reference to the grizzly was a joke between us.

The boisterous greeting was Lonny's way of calling attention to having worked for us. He was proud he had been chief guide on my husband's big game outfitting staff of Indian guides for almost twenty years. Louis and I were just as proud this loyal little Indian had guided for us all those years.

No matter how brutal the trail, muskeg swamps, swollen rivers, blinding snowstorms or freezing rain, if I could see Lonny Johnny's white shirt at the head of the pack train, I knew we would make it through. He always wore a white shirt until one day I caught up with him as he held up the horses to size up the trail ahead. Lonny's white shirt was drenched and his teeth were chattering. From my saddle bag I jerked out my sweater. Lonny drew himself up with dignity and disdainfully refused the offer. I was just as determined I wasn't going to have a guide with pneumonia on my hands. Sticking out my chin and glaring, I declared, "I'm your boss, you wear this sweater or your fired," but I couldn't help giggling.

Lonny lifted one eyebrow, squinting at me, the corners of his mouth twitching. "You my boss. You no see camp, you lost," thumping his chest, "Lonny Johnny no get lost."

We both doubled over our saddle horn, laughing at how ridiculous it was for a raw city cheechako to boss a supreme woodsman of the northern bush. He condescended to wear the sweater and from then on, with his eyes twinkling with merriment, he referred to me as his boss.

A great mountain system known as the North American Cordillera forms a portion of the division between the Northwest Territories and the Yukon. East of the rugged mountains, on the Mackenzie River, are two forts — Fort Good Hope and Fort Norman. Here lived a small tribe of Indians known as the Mountain Indians, to distinguish them from the Indians living around Great Bear Lake. On their hunting expeditions they were careful never to get near the Cordillera divide, for fear of evil spirits, who were gigantic Indians.

According to the 1907 and 1908 geological report by Joseph Keele, these Mountain Indians were of a superior class of men to the surrounding tribes. Lonny Johnny was born into this mountain tribe when they were still very primitive. His cradle was a moose skin sling and he was wrapped in a rabbit skin blanket.

In 1890, Frank Braine, a free white trader, induced some of this tribe to cross the feared divide into the Yukon and established them on the Stewart River, at the mouth of Lancing creek, where he erected a fur trading post. Later, when Lonny was but a small boy, he made this trek across the Mackenzie Mountains to the Lancing trading post.

Lonny Johnny became unequalled in the Northern bush. Once over a trail, he never forgot it. He knew every tone of a wolf's howl and knew what it meant. He knew the habits of the wilderness creatures and could mimic them perfectly. He had extensive knowledge of the wild medicinal plants and was adept in their use. Although Lonny had never even heard of a psychologist, he himself was an expert in using tact and diplomacy to deal with a difficult hunter or a grumbling guide. Seldom did Lonny loose his patience, but when he did and called some hunter "Dumb White Man", he did it in such a way they were highly amused and never took offence.

About 1938, my husband, Louis, met Lonny Johnny at Lancing's trading post and they trapped together for several years. During this time, Louis learned the required skills to become an accomplished Northern woodsman and Lonny could think of no greater praise than to say: "Louis, all same Indian."

In 1947, when Louis took up Big game guiding and became an

outfitter, Lonny joined his staff of Indian guides and I met him when Louis and I were married. To change a Washington State secretary into a big game guide was a task Lonny unconsciously took on. To say our diverse cultures baffled both each other would be an under statement. By turns, Lonny Johnny fascinated and infuriated me. The many instances of my ignorance and stupidity were always met equably and with jolly good humor.

Lonny's philosophy was a thorn in my side and completely in opposition to the way I wanted to react to bodily discomforts. If a horse stepped on my toe I wanted to scream, but Lonny was determined to teach me that no matter what happened I was to be cheerful. At first I balked. How could I be cheerful when a horse bucked me onto a pile of rocks and it hurt like blazes? How could I be cheerful when the packtrain ran over a hornets nest and most stung me to death? How could I be cheerful when I was frozen stiff in the saddle? However, Lonny, going through even greater discomforts and hardships, met it all with good humor, even to laughing and joking about it. This made me grind my teeth because I knew if I gave vent to tears over some mishap, Lonny would make fun of me and have the whole staff of guides laughing. Yet, if I were in real danger, they were quick to be by my side.

Lonny was also determined to teach me the impracticality of worry. The first time I ran against this side of his philosophy was during my first year of marriage. Louis had taken a party of his hunters on a side trip and didn't return when he was expected. I was frantic. I had lost my new husband. I rushed out of the cook tent to confront Lonny. "Something terrible has happened to Louis or he would be back by now. Go at once and see if you can find him."

Lonny gave me a penetrating look, shaking his head as if he couldn't believe any one would make such a fuss over a matter so inconsequential. He decided he better try and reason with me. "Why you worry? He alright, he have lots matches, lots shells, big gun, he OK."

Gradually, Lonny's philosophy began to sink in, but it was extremely difficult to discipline myself to the toughness and self control needed to face calmly the many dangers one confronts when riding the big game trails of the Northern wilderness. If I hadn't learned the many lessons from Lonny, I wouldn't be alive today. It took the training Lonny drilled into me to stand twelve feet from a grizzly without a gun and not panic, not to mention the sixteen other grizzlies I was later to confront.

Equally important was to learn the habits of the big game. I think when Lonny's training did me the most good was when a grizzly kept me up a cache all night and I had only one shell in my gun. Instead of taking a chance of shooting in the dark, I waited under siege for daylight and killed him with my last shell.

This led up to the joke between Lonny Johnny and me. The hunting party had been gone for several days and I had been alone in camp. I had just killed the grizzly when the hunting party returned. Lonny said later, he had been scared when he was in sight of camp and there was no smoke. He rode ahead of the party and began shouting: "YOU OK? YOU OK?"

"Yes," I yelled back, "but I'm not sure if this grizzly is entirely dead."

Lonny said later that when he heard this, his hair stood on end and he raced his horse to where I was trying to climb down from the cache. In haste, he jumped from the horse with his gun cocked, ready for fast action. When he saw the grizzly stretched out at the foot of the cache, he yelled "JESUS CHRIST!" and then, to my astonishment, Lonny started dancing around the grizzly yelling "BEAR ALMOST GET ME! BOSS SAVE ME! BOSS SAVE ME!"

By now the hunting party was standing around with mouths agape and speechless, while Lonny kept dancing and yelling "BOSS SHOOT'M DAMN GOOD! SAVE THIS INDIAN!"

At times Lonny's sense of humor took some odd twists. Once, after a big game hunt and we were in town, I heard Lonny Johnny yelling up the street. "HELP BOSS! BOSS HELP!"

Lonny ran up to me breathless. "Boss, guy stole my money."

"Where is he Lonny?"

Lonny pointed. "He go around corner."

"Don't worry, Lonny, I'll get your money back." I dashed around the corner and slammed up against a big, burley Swede, all of six foot four tall.

Lonny yelled: "That him! THAT HIM!"

Before demanding Lonny's money back, I desperately looked around for Louis. My husband wasn't in sight. Gaining my courage, I felt maybe tact would be the best approach. "I believe you have misappropriated my guide's money?"

"He's a damn liar!" The Swede, rum drunk, glared at me.

I looked around for Lonny to substantiate his claim, but Lonny had sneaked back around the corner convulsed with laughter. When I caught up with him, he was choking with mirth. "OH, boss! Your face so funny when you see that big guy."

Because of his good natured humor, Lonny was a great favorite with the hunters. He could even rib them over their poor shooting and get away with it.

Beneath Lonny's jokes and good humor there was a formality and dignity that revealed a strength of character which demanded respect, and every big game hunter he guided recognized this little Indian's worth.

Lonny's artistic nature always fascinated me. He loved to carve ram horns into different articles. My favorite being a beautiful large soup spoon

Once, riding out of the high country, we came upon two moose with their horns locked in death. After we scared away the grizzly that was feeding on it, Lonny was quick to size up their potential and artistically formed the two sets of horns into a huge picture frame. He then had each member of the party pose to have their picture taken in this primitive frame.

Lonny had a fantastic inner compass that guided him unerringly over the most rugged terrain. He was the only guide who never forgot a trail.

Years ago Sven Johanson, a big game outfitter working over on the Arctic Red River before there was road access, hired Lonny to deliver some horses from Mayo to his base camp. The trip was a very hazardous undertaking. Lonny hadn't been over the old Indian trail since he was a very small boy, when he came over the Divide to Lancing Post. Weather and new growth had obliterated much of it. Game trails were covered by mud and rock slides caused by winter avalanches. There were treacherous rivers to cross and what maps existed were sketchy and unreliable.

Surviving great hardships and dangers, Lonny guided the horses across uncharted mountain ranges and with uncanny skill led them safely to the outfitter's camp at Arctic Red River, proving the caliber of this little Indian as a superior Northern woodsman.

Once one of Lonny's hunters got excited and lost his cool when a grizzly charged down a mountain. With a terrified yell, the hunter threw down his gun and leaped behind Lonny for protection. Lonny had no choice but to shoot the grizzly and it fell dead at their feet.

Afterwards the hunter went to Louis in fear that his cowardly action would be exposed to his hunting pals and with shame asked, "will Lonny tell my buddies?"

Louis, an admirer of the famous Northern poet Charles E. Gillham, remembered a line from one of his poems and quoted, "Hell no, he's your guide."

Lonny guided many famous big game hunters and he himself became famous as a superior guide. At times, my desk was flooded with requests for Lonny to guide hopeful hunters. Even after a hunt, letters kept coming inquiring about the welfare of our chief guide.

At the start of a hunt, Lonny brought only a small dunnage bag. At the end of the hunting season it required several dunnage bags to hold all the gifts appreciative hunters gave him.

In 1987, when Louis lay dying, he wanted to console me. "Don't worry. Lonny will be waiting with the pack train of the wonderful horses who have gone before us and we'll travel new trails."

Prominent natural land marks now carry their names, reminding future generations that Louis and Lonny were two of Yukon's most famous big game guides.

Even now, years after their deaths, letters still come to me claiming they are now a legend. Wonderful examples of good sportsmanship and integrity, they are to the Yukon what Daniel Boone was to the West.

Chapter 18

WHO'S TRESPASSING ON MY TRAPLINE?

(By Louis Brown)

I'm willing to bet a stack of beaver pelts that when Robert Service, the famous Bard of the North, wrote his immortal lines about the cremation of Sam McGee, he had no idea there would be queerer sights to see in this sub-Arctic than the stuffing of McGee into the furnace at Lake Lebarge.

I've a strong hunch old Sam would have fled the furnace had he seen what I saw that night the Aurora Borealis played hop scotch on the peaks of Hungry Mountain, here in Central Yukon.

I'm a trapper and I'm use to moody wilderness, lonely camps, and weird displays of Northern Lights, but it didn't prepare me for the phenomena I saw that night in October, several years ago.

I had nothing more important on my mind than thinking about a trapper's steady income yield, the Canadian Sable, better known as Martin. The weather had been cold enough to make the pelts prime, the fur market was good and I had been lucky.

The week before, just above timberline, I had killed a moose. After gutting and skinning it out, I had made a pile of the quarters, spread the heavy skin over the meat, and then shoveled plenty of snow on top to keep off the Ravens.

Two days later I returned with my toboggan to haul the meat down to the cabin. I found the whole area covered with Martin tracks, so I set several Martin traps instead.

In less than a week I picked up eight large, dark, almost black, Martin, the very best. It was too late to load the sled with the moose meat, so I slipped back down to a thick stand of Balsam. The trees bordered a wide, deep ravine, which gave a sweeping view of the valley below and also a wide expanse of sky. The Northern Lights were beginning to play when I wearily dove into my Eddy Bauer sleeping bag.

Sometime during the night I was awakened with what seemed to be points of light flickering across my eye lids. Half asleep I opened my eyes, then sat bolt upright and gasped in amazement at the awesome activity in space. The sky was full of stars running amuck. Thousands of blazing blobs of lights were travelling at incredible speed, horizontally and vertically across the blue blackness of night. I've watched satellites hundreds of times, but they never reversed in mid sky nor have meteorites I've seen shoot back up into the sky after blinking out on the horizon.

If it was a natural phenomenon, they certainly left it out of any book I had ever read on astronomy. No machine on earth could maneuver at those speeds without falling apart, but if they weren't stars or machines then what in hell were they?

Shafts of Aurora Borealis now darted among the activated stars, bringing to mind what Service had written, that they would see such queer sights it would make your blood run cold. Only my blood froze.

Had I known that a few years later, in February of 1978, I was going to see an even queerer sight in our night sky, I think as soon as I got off the mountain I would have caught a fast jet to New York City, where you can't see the stars and the lights on Broadway don't scare hell out of you.

Seriously, it was no joke. It was not only eerie but also perplexing. I watched until dawn. Sleep was forgotten and so was the meat. I wanted to find out fast whether my wife, Dolores, had seen what I was seeing. The way I drove those huskies, I could easily have won the thousand mile Iditarod race from Anchorage to Nome in five days.

One look at my face and Dolores anxiously asked: "What's the matter?"

"Did you see anything strange last night?" I hurriedly questioned.

"Should I have?"

After I described the happenings of the night, Dolores laughed. "Oh, Louis, you were dreaming."

"I was NOT. I even got out of my sleeping bag to make sure I was awake."

"Then you saw UFOs."

It was my turn to laugh. "The only people who see UFOs are the neurotics."

138

"Then you're neurotic."

"ME...ME..neurotic? NEVER!"

"Then you saw UFOs."

I just couldn't accept the idea of UFOs, but it kept worrying me. What had I seen?

I had to go to Mayo for some trapping supplies. Danny Jurovich, the owner of the General Mercantile store, was a no-nonsense, crack businessman and I knew I could depend on Danny. He wasn't busy, so we had a chance to gab. I took some time before I could screw up enough courage to ask "Danny, have you ever seen strange lights in the sky?"

"I sure have."

That stopped me cold "You've really seen stars streaking across...?"

"No, but I've seen a big glowing light that turned the snow blue and stopped my car engine."

By the time Danny got through describing his encounter with what he assumed to be a UFO, which had petrified him, I wasn't sure what to believe. I knew damn well Danny wasn't neurotic.

Reports began hitting me from all directions. Cecile Curry, wife of one of the staff members of Keno Hill's silver mines, was looking out her window at the vast uninhabited wilderness when she spotted three globes of orange lights, each about the size of the moon. "It terrified me. I don't want to even think about it," she said.

A big game outfitter, hunting over on the Bonnet Plume River area next to the border of the Northwest Territories, spotted a large, pulsing light hovering over a pyramid-shaped mountain. Having trapped in that area for many years, I knew the area well and that the mountain had titanium, a mineral the UFOs needed, according to one English woman I read about later who claimed contact with one of the space astronauts.

Gus and Nellie Burgelman, mining and trapping over on Caribou Creek, kept seeing strange stars with strange misty glow that didn't act like stars.

Sighting reports kept piling up, but as to their identity, there were only suppositions and I wanted hard-nosed, concrete facts, so I dropped the whole subject until one night. Arriving home late from a stint on my longest line with a load of lynx, I happened to glance toward Hungry Mountain in time to see an unusual light that was so bright, it had the blinding brilliance of a welding torch, but of gigantic size. With incredible speed it came down at an angle. Below the sky-line, it made a sharp reverse turn and took off up a draw, showing the scar of a fault.

I almost broke down the door getting to Dolores, to tell her of the awesome sight. She shook her head, said nothing but gave me a long look that made me wonder if my wife thought I had gone bush.

After that, I noticed she spent a great deal of time at night outside, even when temperatures were way below the zero mark. I wondered if she was trying to find proof of my sanity or insanity. So it was a relief when one night she excitedly called, "LOUIS...HURRY...HURRY.. COME OUT HERE!".

I knew by that excited tone she had seen something; hopefully something which would exonerate me. She pointed at a small star, slowly moving up from the horizon.

I voiced my opinion "Must be a satellite."

"No, wait. See....?"

The small star was heading straight for a very large star directly over our heads. We waited for it to pass, but when we saw the smaller star again, it was returning to the horizon. I had the lynx to skin, so I left Dolores to stand vigil. She kept shouting reports that were so fantastic, I finally threw down the skinning knife and joined her.

Sometimes several smaller stars from different directions traveled to a much larger star and then they took off, the smaller stars no longer in sight.

Neither of us had the courage to ask the other if extraterrestrials might be coming to look us over. Instead, we bought astronomy and science books.

Night after night, while I skinned fur, Dolores read to me. To our anxious minds, it seemed the scientists were as mixed up as we were. Even our favorite scientists were coming to some wrong conclusions. In 1899, Nikola Tesla thought he'd picked up electrical signals of extraterrestrial origin. Later, his colleagues thought more likely he was tuning in on natural emissions from Earth's magnetic field.

It was a little heartening when we found out that Carl Sagan, director of Cornell University's Laboratory for Planetary studies, believed one star in a million could support advanced civilizations.

Nobelist Gerhard Herzburg, of Canada's National Research Council, seems to agree. He thinks it would be very strange if there weren't other planetary systems like ours among the 100 billion stars in the Milky Way.

However, as far as we were concerned, these opinions were no spectacular breakthrough. Way back in the Fourth Century BC, the old Greek philosopher Metrodorus of Chios thought: "To consider the Earth the only populated world in infinite space is as absurd as to assert that in an entire field sown with seed, only one grain will grow."

Dolores was of the opinion: "Louis, if old Metrodorus wasn't afraid to speak out, why can't you tell people you just might be seeing extraterrestrials?"

"Not on your life, you just read where a few centuries later Giordano Bruno was burned alive at the stake for espousing theories similar to Metrodorus."

"Maybe it's little green men" Dolores teased.

"Well, just keep on reading until you find out what in hell they're doing on my trapline."

Because we found there were unprecedented numbers of serious, high-profile astronomers, physicists, and space technologists lending serious credence to theories of inhabited worlds, we kept on watching the night skies.

Then, on the last Sunday of February of 1978, about 8pm on an evening of minus forty-six degree temperatures, it happened.

That afternoon we had crossed the Stewart River to a smaller trapping cabin to trap for wolf. The wolf population was exceeding the game supply and a balance in nature's ratio was badly needed. All afternoon we had heard the moaning of the packs.

Because of the low temperature, the cabin was taking a long time to warm up. Dolores had snuggled early into her Eddy Bauer sleeping robe. Before turning in, I went to the door to check if there were any weather moderating clouds in sight. Carefully scanning the night skies, my eyes suddenly focused sharply on an immense star, only it just didn't look right for a star. For one thing, it was about three times larger than any visible star. Secondly, it wasn't even clear of the treetops. Having become an inveterate stargazer, I certainly would have noticed it before. For some reason I kept thinking: "I want to see you move...I want to see you move..."

Suddenly I felt electrical prickles going up and down my neck as the thing began to pulse in a fiery glow and damned if it didn't move about three hundred yards horizontally west and stopped.

I yelled to Dolores. "Bring my binoculars! QUICK!"

Dolores leaped out of bed and I grabbed my 9 x 35 Bausch & Lomb, not taking my eyes off the oscillating light.

141

"Do you see that star near the pass?" I asked my wife.

"Louis, I don't think it is a star, it's too big and I've never seen a star behind the trees before."

"Watch....watch close. I just saw it move."

"I ... I can't...I'm freezing" my wife shivered and jumped back into bed missing a wonderful chance to see the star turn into a glowing ball of pulsating fire. I had the damnedest feeling something inside that light was watching me. Then the glow begun to expand and it took off with incredible speed up through the pass. It went behind the highest peak of Hungry Mountain then, appearing again, it sped out of sight.

The next day I made a trip into Mayo to see the Royal Canadian (Mounted) police. I asked the Corporal: "Did you see any unusual light in the sky last night?"

"Why yes, some of the boys reported seeing a strange light when they were travelling between the Pelly and Stewart rivers." Then he went on to describe what I had seen.

I have never read science fiction, nor have I seen Star Wars and my imagination wouldn't even pass muster with a six-year-old wearing a space suit. My heroes are the great hunters of history. They were and are a different breed of men, driven by an ardent desire to achieve, to test their courage, resourcefulness, strength, and endurance. Long before the Green Peacers were wearing diapers, it was the hunters who put their money where their mouths were and built game reserves and game sanctuaries.

Theirs has been a great heritage, spanning centuries, with hunter forebears developing in the hunter a keenness of observation, awareness, and courage that made them the vanguards of every new frontier.

I believe this phenomena has created a new dimension for the dedicated,

A genuine hunter, being a superb tracker, may lift his eyes from the wilderness of continents and scan the skies with the same intensity, eagerness, and expectancy as when in pursuit of game. This time, his success in exploring a new frontier may be among the stars.

Chapter 19

WOLF, SAINT OR SINNER?

(By Louis Brown)

The spine chilling moaning of the wolves was somewhere ahead, but the shifting wind made it impossible to pinpoint the exact location of the pack. The driving frost crystals increased to such an intensity it was like a white window shade being drawn, blotting out most of the light. Because of the low temperature, almost fifty below, I wore extra large moose skin mukluks stuffed with fox fur, a pair of fur beaver mitts and heavy caribou parka with a hood edged in a double wolverine ruff. It made a pretty clumsy outfit for riding.

Sweetheart, my wife's small mare, was a mixture of Arab, Welsh, and pure Cayuse cussedness, but she was smart enough to know where every Marten trap was set. In the blinding snow I had to depend on her and she never missed one. However, she was getting nervous and whenever I bent down to reset a trap, she kept nudging me to hurry.

At the top of Hungry Mountain, where the line ended, Sweetheart didn't need me to tell her to head for home. She plunged down the steep ridge, making it impossible to keep my mukluks in the stirrups. We both were glad to be leaving the wolf packs behind. I didn't like the idea of running into a large bunch when visibility was so poor.

Half way down the mountain, Sweetheart lunged to the side of the trail. Looking down I saw fresh tracks of a moose in full flight, followed by the tracks of three wolves. Poor devil, a clean shot would be more merciful than falling under the fangs of those butchers of hell.

We worked on down the mountain. I drew my face into the protection of the wolverine ruff and let the mare pick her own way. I knew I could trust her for she was headed for a pail of oats waiting for her in the log barn.

As Sweetheart jogged along, I couldn't keep my mind from worrying about disturbing reports. Each year I had watched the packs getting larger and more numerous. As a result, the wild game here was dwindling alarmingly.

I remembered the time I was camped over on the Bonnet Plume River with a hunting party when a chopper landed with two very distraught pilots. A couple of hours earlier they had landed up river on a sand bar and were unpacking their gear when a couple of wolves attacked them. One of the pilots shot them. Later, when reporting the incident to headquarters, they were sent back to collect the heads, but all they found were more wolf tracks. I believe there was only one thing that could have caused such action on the part of the wolves and it made me shudder.

If old Mother Nature was using her own method to bring the wolves under control, then we were in one hell of a lot of trouble. I don't think anything can be much worse than an epidemic of hydrophobia.

Sweetheart suddenly reared, bringing me out of the parka hood with a jerk. We had dropped down to the edge of a bench overlooking a small lake that was shallow enough in summer to attract moose, who feed on the tender shoots of aquatic plants, and a great place for muskrat hunting in the spring. Wanting to set more muskrat traps, I lead the little mare down a game trail to the lake. Much to my relief, the skies were clearing and it had stopped snowing. Just as we reached shore ice, Sweetheart threw up her head, snorted and stood trembling. Her ears pointed to the far end of the lake. I could see some dark objects. Grabbing my 9x35 Bausch & Lomb binoculars, I hurriedly focused. The glasses picked up an awesome sight. The wolf pack. Big black fellows. I'm used to counting cattle on the range and estimating the numbers of migrating caribou herds and I was pretty sure there were all of forty wolves on the ice and, from the waving of the nearby willow thicket, I was sure there were more that I couldn't see. There wasn't a grey or white wolf among them. I've seen a lot of wolf packs, but never before all of one color. Those jet-black devils loomed menacingly against the white background.

They must have heard and scented me for miles. Years ago they would have run like hell, but these wolves didn't give a damn. One lone howl and they started trotting towards me. Snatching my 30-30 Winchester out of the scabbard, I was shoving a shell into the chamber when Sweetheart screamed and whirled, the shell jammed. With a plunging, terrified horse, I was unable to do anything with the gun. A

144

quick glance backwards, the wolves had cut the distance by half. I decided the only thing to do was get the hell out of there. By the time I mounted the plunging horse in my bulky arctic clothing, the wolves had drawn even closer. Sweetheart took off on a dead run and never slowed down until we were in sight of the barn. We could still hear the wolves howling when I tucked her safely by the manger with her reward of oats.

That evening Dolores, my wife, was highly amused when I took down every high powered rifle I owned, cleaned and oiled them and carefully checked the trigger action. I had made up my mind. In the morning, I was going back after that wolf pack with plenty of shells and traps and cut its size down to reasonable numbers. Just imagine how much game a pack that large can eat during a winter! Flint, one of our huskies, ate a whole horse by himself in only one month.

Early the next morning I started out with Tammy, a three-year-old, carrying pack boxes loaded with traps and shells. Sweetheart carried scabbards holding a 308 Savage and a 270 Winchester. I wasn't a mile from the cabin when both horses went crazy, bucking, lunging and frantically trying to head back. I was having my hands full when I heard two shots. It meant Dolores was using her 270 Winchester and she only used it when she meant business. Worried she might be in trouble, I reined the horses around and they streaked it for home. I arrived just in time to see Dolores run across a snowbank over looking the U-slough. About forty feet below on the ice, two wolves were tucking in their tails, zig zagging with bellies hugging the ice. Another shot, she missed again. Before I could get within range, the wolves disappeared into the brush.

"You were shooting high," I told her.

"I know, I lost the gold bead on my sights and I can't see good in this white-out."

We could hear the wolves howling all around. No use going looking for them, they had found me. I took both horses down to the slough to water them. Tammy started snorting and stood staring. About two hundred yards from us a grey wolf hunkered on the ice watching us. I hurriedly tied the horses to a spruce tree, ran up the trail to the cabin for my 308, and dashed back to the edge of the bank. I snapped off a couple of shots. The wolf sprang up and disappeared in the bordering brush. Jumping down the steep bank and finding splotches of light colored blood indicating it to be a lung shot, I followed the tracks. The growing darkness made me uneasy. I might not be able to see a surprise attack, so I went back after my Siberian Husky.

Flint was excited when he smelled blood and was keenly alert. We both clawed our way through a tangle of willow, Hudson Bay tea and wild rise bushes. We caught up to where the wounded wolf lay down for a short time. He was travelling slowly. When a sharp staccato bark sounded near, Flint and I both jumped. Low moaning grew into excited yips. The wolves surrounded us. Being a trapper, I knew I had to reach my quarry first if its prime pelt was to be saved. I scuttled through the dense under growth until coming to an old logging road, then jumped up and ran. Ten yards ahead was a horrendous sight. Torn pieces of grey fur and blood littered a large area of trampled snow. The pack had no mercy and the pelt was a total loss.

Even though it was late, I had to hitch up the team of horses and go after some much-needed firewood. I had been putting it off because the team I used for hauling had been acting strangely, as if they were having fits. Reluctantly I hitched up the two horses and threw several marten carcasses on the bobsled to dispose. Never having known wolves to eat Martin, I felt safe the carcasses wouldn't attract them.

Yelling to Dolores "JUMP ON, they won't stand", I unsnubbed. The team took the fence post with them when they lunged and we were off in a flurry of snow. In a quarter of a mile the road forked, forming a V with both branches eventually connecting to the old historical stage road used by the great and not so great characters of the 1898 Klondike gold rush.

The team was so wild it was hard to get them to take the left branch and when we hit the stage road, Dolores dumped the carcasses. A mile further we turned into the wood lot.

As soon as the horses were tied, they flopped down and kicked all eight hoofs into the air. Dolores shook her head apprehensively "I think we better load fast."

"We'll have to reinforce the bed of the sled first with long spruce poles," I told her. We didn't take time to shorten the poles so they hung down over the end of the bobsled, which later proved a good thing.

A long, low mournful howl, pierced the ice fog made by the heavily breathing horses. We stopped to listen, WOLVES!

We speedily finished the loading and Dolores climbed on top of the load, while I worked to get the horses back on their feet. I knew as soon as they were up they'd have to have their heads or they'd flop back down. Yanking the hitching rope loose, I yelled "HANG ON!"

We hit the stage road with a lurch that almost upset us on the turn When we neared the turn off I began to see wolf tracks. A full moon came from behind the clouds, making it almost as light as day. Ahead I saw slinking shadows. The wolves were feeding on the Martin carcasses.

There was no other way but past them. I yelled to frighten them but it only sent the team into a full gallop and the wolves only moved back into the willows.

The team whiplashed the bobsled off the stage road onto the cut off and out of the corner of my eye I saw wood and Dolores fly off the load. I couldn't stop the horses and I couldn't leave my wife back with the wolves.

See-sawing on the lines I slowed the team down enough to swing them onto the other branch of the road and circled back to the stage road. As I drew close to the carcasses I yelled "GRAB ON! GRAB ON!"

I knew I couldn't slow down enough for Dolores to climb on, but if she was quick enough she might be able to grab the end of a pole. Hurriedly glancing back, I saw my wife clutch a pole, her feet flew out from under her, but she hung on.

Reaching the corral, the team flopped down on the snow, kicking and rolling as if in agony. I ran to the cabin and on our radiophone called the Whitehorse vet. The sum of our conversation being that I was feeding them sweet clover hay that was mouldy and it was poisoning them, causing fits. After a couple of weeks on good alfalfa hay, they fully recovered.

Spring would surely bring the end of our wolf problems, so it was with relief when I heard the booming, crunching of ice on the mighty Stewart River heralding the beginning of spring.

We were shocked when an Indian came to tell us one of our heifers had leaped over the bluff and was trapped on a ledge only a foot above the raging torrent of ice, drifting logs, and up rooted trees. We hurried to the river. Now she was only inches above the rush of ice and flooding debris. On the other side of her was a perpendicular bank, eighty feet of sheer wall. The only way of rescue was to dig steps. We raced with time digging the steps, fearful the huge chunks of floating ice would push her into the swollen river before we could complete hacking out the stairway. Five feet from the top of the bank the river was swirling around her legs and we waited no longer. Pulling and pushing we got her to the last step, then dragged her to the top. We then found the reason for her terrified leap. Wolf tracks.

We thought she would be safe in the corral, but in the morning she was gone and the Indians told us the same heifer was back over the same bluff. It meant the wolves had picked this one animal and would keep after her until they killed her, as was their habit. At least we had the steps already cut and hauled her out again. Next day, on her way to water with the herd, the wolves dragged her down only a hundred yards from the barn.

At one in the morning I was awakened by piercing scream from a terrified animal. Rushing out with my 30-30 I was in time to see a wolf crawling after a calf that had sought safety underneath the tractor. I was to late to save the calf, but the wolf made a fine rug in front of the fireplace.

With summer came sweeping fires throughout the Yukon Territory. The wolf packs moved into settled areas and neighbours were losing chickens, rabbits, and dogs. When Annie Lee, one of our prized registered Scotch Highland cows didn't show up, I went looking for her. She was ready to calve and I didn't want to lose such a valuable animal. When I returned Dolores anxiously asked "Did you find her?"

"Yea, I found her. She must have been one helluva a fighter. Willows and brush was smashed down for a radius of fifty feet. Tracks showed there were all of nine wolves. She didn't have a chance."

I don't hate wolves. I just want them kept in balance. The North would lose the romance and thrill of the wilderness without the vocal challenge of a wolf's lonely howl on some distant ridge. The primitive in us answers the call with deeply felt longings for the same freedom. It stirs within us a burning desire to be released from the pressures of civilization. It restores us to Life's basic simplicity of living.

The wolf is a symbol of freedom, and like freedom they must be in balance. Throughout the years there have been assertions that the wolf was becoming extinct. Let me reassure those who have this fear that the wolf population is healthy and, as long as Brown's beef lasts, they will never become extinct.

Chapter 20

CACHE IT IN THE YUKON

Under the shadow of the Arctic Circle, in the middle of two hundred and seven thousand square miles of permafrost, scattered along remote rivers and hidden valleys, are the Yukon's equivalent to Chase and Manhattan banks. That is, if you consider a bank as a place to deposit your valuables. Old sourdoughs considered them safer than the citadels of Wall Street.

The caches of the Yukon are noted for their bizarre deposits including everything from dental forceps to dynamite. Running competition to Fort Knox, they also contain an assortment of rusty tin cans filled with the most famous commodity of the Yukon, GOLD, in dust to pebble size nuggets. Stranger yet, greenbacks of assorted denominations have been found in the moss chinking. One year we came across an old prospector whose sub Arctic bank had leaked. Ten, fifty and hundred dollar bills were spread over logs, rocks, and stumps, drying out under the evaporating rays of a hot sun.

Since Yukon caches have saved my life twice, I consider them more important than Canada's Imperial Bank of Commerce.

The design of a cache depends on the necessity and urgency to deposit. There are tree caches, log caches, suspension caches, and rock caches, but the most popular and romantic are the stilt caches. They are built on four trees, (if they can be found close together) sawed off between eight to twelve feet in height. On these four posts is built a pole platform. If it is a deluxe style, a small log cabin is erected on the platform.

Like any bank, they are built with a safeguard, usually a tin garter around each post. This forestalls any run on the bank by martin, mink, mice or squirrels, but no safety measures can make them entirely burglar proof, for roaming the Yukon wilderness is one expert who can bust any of these bush banks. He is noted for chewing through a post, then ramming the splintered post until the whole cache crashes.

I once had first hand evidence as to how he does it. I was on top of the cache when a grizzly spent the night trying to chew it down. At one point we were eye to eye. After four hours of chewing, he grew tired and stood up full length to see if the meal screeching on top was worth all the effort, and I was looking down through the pole platform to check on what progress he was making. It was dark and when I shone my flashlight down, I almost fell off the cache to discover we were within kissing distance.

As late as the middle of the nineteen hundreds, parts of the Yukon were so remote that government maps were sketchy. So, in our big game hunting areas of the Wind, Bonnet Plume and Snake rivers, we bestowed names on some of the nameless rivers and lakes, usually relating to some cache in the vicinity.

Whiskey Creek was where we found a tree cache with a bottle of whiskey that had been aging there for over forty years.

Rascal Creek was where a little black bear followed me up the cache ladder, helped himself to moose steaks I was cutting, then scampered back into the brush before I was aware of the theft.

Bean Creek cache held nothing but beans. Enough kegs of white, brown, and spotted beans to have supplied the whole horde of Genghis Khan on their ride across latitudes. Those early day banking tycoons were surely full of beans.

Loon Creek cache is where I learned not all demonic sounds come from demons. We were camped on the shore of Fairchild Lake next to a swaying two-pole cache. Before leaving for the day's hunt, my husband warned me: "You can't climb that cache, so don't try. Your curiosity can wait until I find time to knock together a ladder. Mostly moose horns up there anyway."

Left alone, I walked around the cache several times, deciding Louis was right. It would be impossible to climb. I was enjoying nature's beauty, when an eerie, terrifying sound split the silence. How I wished I was back in the city. Another wild blood-chilling cry, closer this time, and in one second flat I was on top of the cache. Looking around to see from what direction the attack would come, I saw a bird in the water calmly diving. It was uniquely marked in black and white. I was admiring its plumage when another weird cry echoed across the lake. I was shocked to see it was coming out of the mouth of that beautiful bird. I have since learned to love the cry of the loon.

Dolores Creek has been officially recognized on the Government maps of the Yukon Territory. Anyone looking at the wavy black line representing a dashing, winding expanse of grey, green water would never guess that in one of its twisty turns nestles a dilapidated cache, so old, arctic spruce grow densely around it, almost obliterating it from sight and making it dark and spooky. It was very late in the afternoon when the hunting party left me alone to guard the camp and explore the cache.

The big find was an old rounded top steamer trunk, full of red wool long johns and socks full of holes. I was busy rummaging, paying no attention to the growing nervousness of seven horses tied close to the cache. When two of the horses broke loose, their hobbles clanging off into the darkness, I slid down the pole and hurriedly built a fire. When the horses started screaming and struggling to get loose, I piled more logs on the fire. In spite of his arthritis, old Dan broke loose and jumped the fire, raced under the cache, knocking loose one of it's supporting poles. Ginger followed screaming in terror. I headed back up the pole ladder with the speed no fireman could equal.

Just as I clawed to the platform, a silvertip grizzly stalked into the circle of light. He sniffed the gun I had forgotten, but wasn't interested. Slowly lifting one huge paw after the other, he edged closer to the cache. It was then I realized how much lower than all the others this cache had been built. The grizzly knew I was up there, because every time he stopped to sniff, he looked straight at me. His eyes showed too much intelligence to be reassure me he wasn't thinking about a meal. I crawled behind the small cabin, hoping to be out of sight, out of mind. Curious to know what had happened to the creature on top, he came closer, standing up full length, leaning against the cache, tilting the platform. I fought to calm my nerves as the cache was wobbly enough without me shaking it. The grizzly was alert to every sound and I tried not to move. A stick snapped and he growled. The only horse remaining tied stood like a statue. I started to shift my cramping leg, a board squeaked, the grizzly snapped his teeth as if giving a warning. I froze. The silence grew ghastly. I could even hear my wrist watch ticking.

Just when I thought my nerves were going to come unglued, the hunting party burst into the clearing. The grizzly dropped down, and disappeared into the thick brush.

My husband dismounted, yelled "DOLORES"!

I couldn't answer because my vocal cords were stuck.

Another bellow from Louis and I managed to squeak "Here."

Louis looked astonished. "What in hell are you doing up there when the horses are loose?"

"What in the hell do you think? Look at those tracks."

Louis started laughing. "Never thought a little old bear could chase a chief guide up a cache!"

Still trembling with fright and infuriated over my husband's lack of concern over the danger, I jumped up stamping my feet and the whole cache crashed.

The flea markets of Paris are tame compared to the loot found on Yukon caches. One late fall, riding a remote and rugged trail, we came upon a three legged cache, shakily balancing a diminutive, decaying log cabin with one of Edison's first morning glory horns sticking through the rotting roof. We quickly rescued the old phonograph and were astonished it still ran, after all the years of snow and below freezing temperatures.

It was as exciting as being given a free ticket to the Met when we found a whole box of round cylinder disks. There were groans of disappointment when I told the gang they were all operas.

It was a grubby audience of guides, wranglers, and big game hunters sitting around a spruce campfire, gnawing on roasted moose ribs. At first, they listened as if they were about to eat pickled eels.

Wagner's Ride of the Valkyries broke the ice. Old Dan, breaking loose and dashing through camp, added to the sound effect of the ride. When one of the hunters told of seeing the opera in Berlin with live horses and a real bonfire on the stage, we were hooked and couldn't wait for the next disk.

Madam Schummen Helt's powerful voice, singing Puccine's Tosca, drowned out the lamentive howls of the wolf pack coming down the river.

Caruso, singing Vesti La Guibba, could never have sung before a more magnificent back drop than the night's dazzling, pink and lavender shower burst of Northern Lights.

Though Jimmy the wrangler loudly voiced his preference for Elvis Presley, he admitted the music of those famous opera stars of the past was more fitting to the mood of the Northern wilderness than Elvis.

We decided the provider of this unexpected concert must have been a gold rush stampeder. During the dash to the Klondike in the late eighteen hundreds, some came through what is known as the back door to the Yukon, which is in part of our hunting area. In fact, on one of the high passes we found several of their names carved on a board. Finding themselves overburdened, they built caches and unloaded the most fantastic collection of unusable items for their trek to the North.

Through the years I kept checking Whiskey Creek. I had big plans for that aging bottle of Whiskey. I had attached a note, pleading for its survival intact.

In 1934, when my husband first came to the Yukon, he had found some of the old caches still standing, but many had fallen in decay. One intriguing find was where three caches, when collapsing, had flung an amazing assortment of supplies over acres of caribou moss and brush. Louis couldn't believe his eyes when he picked up such things as surgical instruments and dental forceps, hundreds of miles from any civilization.

When I came in 1953 and was taken to this place, it was as much fun as hunting for Easter eggs to still find hidden in the moss old ammunition, such as 38-56s, 45-90s, 40-82s.

The unusual assortment of medical equipment found in such a remote and unpopulated area remained a puzzling mystery until I met an old free white trader. I tell about it in my book, Bonnet Plumes Gold.

Another unusual find was when Louis, coming into the Yukon by the back door and far away from any habitation, investigated an old cache and found a homemade bomb. Years later, he learned it was where the RCMP had routed out the Mad Trapper of Rat River, Albert Johnson.

Caches were a very important part of Louis's life when he was trapping. Sometimes not coming out to civilization for two or three years, protecting his supplies was a matter of life or starvation. The Wind and Bonnet Plume river areas abound in big game, with wolves and grizzlies especially a nuisance. Caribou or moose shot for food had to be immediately protected and a cache was the best means of keeping meat safe. Much of the time it was all Louis had to eat. That is why, years later, when we were big game outfitting, we found so many caches along the game trails of his old trapline.

To me those caches were a God-send. Fresh from a city, at first the Yukon was a big scary place with wild beasts running loose. Many nights when left alone in the hunting camp I slept safely on top of a cache. One night a grizzly thought it his duty to guard the cache. To make sure he wouldn't think about chewing it down, I kept him occupied with eating most of our cached food supplies. He especially liked the butter. When I threw the last pound of two cases down to him, I panicked when he snapped his chops for more.

Being infatuated with caches, Louis built me one for a Christmas present. I consider them more romantic than attics. It's a marvelous place to store all those Christmas and birthday presents you have no idea what to do with. Friends and relatives find it ideal to store discarded evening gowns and clothes they've grown tired of. This has saved me money, for when wanting a new pillow or curtains, I dash for the cache.

A cache provides for endless possibilities in many unexpected ways. Once we ran out of room for visiting guests and a millionaire from Edmonton slept in my cache. Another time a wolf-torn husky, not safe with the rest of our dog team, was kept in the cache until she was well again. Best of all it's a great place to stash forbidden chocolates and all the other sweet goodies from a weight watcher. In extreme moments of stress, it's comforting to know the cache holds a morsel of solace, such as a box of cherry-centered chocolates, to restore faith in the world.

We respect the old caches and when not too decayed, leaky roofs are patched, new poles replace broken platforms, and wobbly posts are given supports. Food is repacked into tins and clothing placed in plastic bags. A tin lined box was especially made to house the old phonograph and cylinders.

Yes, they are the museums of the bush, but they are also the Yukon's bush banks, relics of the days when the most valuable thing you could possess was a keg of beans.

Last year I had a trusted friend check on Whiskey creek. The bottle of whiskey was still aging. It has now been seventy years since it left the big wooden keg of the brewery. Hopefully it won't have to age much longer because what better use for that old, old bottle of whiskey then to toast a celebration of Peace for a tortured planet.

Chapter 21

SKIN BOATS ARE BEST

Any old-time Yukoner will swear on his stack of sourdough flapjacks that a skin boat is one of the finest crafts ever to navigate any northern stream or lake.

Ask him why and he'll snort out a string of adjectives that will leave you dizzy — modifiability, maneuverability, durability, reliability, flexibility, and accessibility. By the time he's through bragging about the superior merits of this most curious natural craft, you'll join him in turning thumbs down to aluminum, fiberglass, plyboard, or any other nonskin boat, for travelling northern rivers.

I know because I married a long time Yukon Territory woodsman, guide, and trapper who is an enthusiastic champion of skin boats. Louis saw his first skin boat in 1933, when he was shooting rapids with far-travelling French voyageurs. Several large Indian families had just descended Gravel River in five skin boats about 30 feet long. The boats were loaded with dog teams, bales of fur, dozens of kids, and other worldly possessions. The durability of these primitive boats made such an impression on Louis that he had some of the Indians teach him the art of building them. He's been making them ever since.

Moose hide was the favorite covering, since the animals were numerous and easy to bring down with bow and arrow. (Sometimes they were snared and then finished off by shooting either with rifle or bow and arrow, or even with a spear.) Occasionally grizzly bear hides were used, but since procuring such a hide was more complicated and dangerous, they were not so popular.

Our friend Lonny Johnny, an Indian who was born in a moose skin tent and who remembers wearing rabbit skin underwear, explains: "Long time ago old people gets grizzly hard way. Takes two fellers. One, him steams ram horn, make it straight, fills him with heavy rock then he hides up tree or rock. Someplace noth'n see him. Other guy get grizzly chase him. He run straight to that feller in tree. That guy in tree jump down on grizzly back and knock him between eyes with ram horn. Bear he go down dead."

Then Lonny Johnny slowly shakes his head and sadly admits: "Sometime guy not so lucky."

There were very few grizzly hide skin boats made in the early days.

When necessary, both types of hides were used. Such was the case with Norman Nidderly, an 80-year-old prospector who took with him a younger man by the name of Klaus Djukastein and flew to Emerald Lake, on the South Fork of the Stewart River.

They had planned to walk out. However, just before time to head home, Norman's bum leg was bothering him, so they decided to come out in a skin boat. They shot one moose but couldn't find another. When an old boar grizzly came pestering around camp, they shot it and made what they called a half-and-half boat — half grizzly, half moose.

The size of a skin boat is never described by dimensions, but rather by the number of skins used. The two-skin boat was most popular, for it was large enough for two trappers and their gear. A four-skin boat could be used for freighting. Louis thinks the boats he first saw on the Mackenzie River must have been made of 10 moose skins each. The accessibility of material and the need determined size.

Spruce roots with a natural lateral bend make the strongest ribs and are usually easiest to procure. In the subarctic, where we live, the permafrost is often just under the moss and spruce roots commonly grow close to the surface so they can be dug out easily.

The slender roots can be chipped into shape with an axe, knife, or even a sharp rock, and they can be lashed to the longitudinal "planking" with rawhide thongs. The best planking for a skin boat is young spruce saplings for they are tough and pliable. Since spruce were hard to get without an axe, the early Indians often used willows.

Nails make a quicker job of building a frame, but rawhide thongs are stronger and have more give and make a far superior boat.

Taking the hair off the skins and fleshing them makes a lighter boat. If building the frame takes too long and the skins become too dry, or if you start with dry skins, soaking them in water for a couple of days brings back the original flexibility and makes it easier to mould the skin around ribs and planking.

Louis built most of his skin boats when there was no limit on game. Nowadays on wilderness trips, if he has room, he packs along a couple of skins of his Scotch Highland cattle, just in case a skin boat is needed.

Once, during the early pre-game law years, when a fancy type of inflatable rubber boat reached the Yukon Territory, Louis decided he had better keep up with modern technology, so he bought one. Since it was going to be a river trip all the way, he took me. We flew to Beaver River, pumped up the expensive fancy creation of modern technology, and started paddling downriver. The Beaver was running swiftly, and sweepers (trees leaning over the river from the bank) rushed past. In less than a mile, a sweeper punched a hole in the boat, and in seconds we were sitting waist deep in ice water.

"Louis," I gasped, "we should have stuck to skin boats."

"Naw. They're old-fashioned. We've got to keep up with the times. They've perfected these boats until they're the best."

"All I know is I never got my pants wet in a skin boat."

After drying out and spending a couple of hours patching, we started out again only to have to stop a couple of miles farther down for another patching job. At about the fifth patch Louis's patience ran out.

"D—! This modern technology could drown you," he grunted as he grabbed his rifle and, with set jaw, strode off between willows.

Next day we had a two-skin boat, and we bounced off willows and rocks like a rubber ball. We scraped harmlessly over rocks, plunged through rapids without shipping a drop, and the two of us could portage the boat with little effort.

Forty-five miles from home we came to Frazier Falls, a treacherous piece of white water where the whole Stewart River shoots between narrow cliffs. The water rolls and boils with frightening speed. No one we have ever heard of has shot this falls in a boat and come out alive. Even most boats allowed to go through alone are splintered to pieces.

We were tired and we didn't want to portage around, so Louis decided to take a chance and send our empty skin boat into the swirling waters. We watched it pitch and plunge into the white-frothed maelstrom, and caught it at the other end, intact. We reloaded it and paddled right to our back door. Louis stepped ashore, tenderly patted the moose hide, and admitted, "I was a fool to think any other kind of boat could ever be as reliable. "

Perhaps the greatest test of the durability of a skin boat came when an Indian family we know well was coming down the Stewart River in their skin boat. One of their children started crying, which attracted a grizzly bear digging for parka squirrels nearby. The bear plunged into the river, swam toward the boat, and reached it before the Indians had collected themselves enough to reach for their guns. The bear gave the boat a tremendous swat, tossing everyone to the bottom of the boat. Before anyone could recover, the grizzly gave it another swipe. Then one of the Indians found his gun and ended the attack.

The grizzly has the strongest forearm of any North American animal, and its claws are long, strong, and sharp. But that skin boat survived without a puncture, the Indians told us, laughing. It didn't leak a drop.

Real old-timers can point out another feature that puts the skin boat at the top of the list over any other boat: if you're ever really up against it for grub, you can always boil and eat a skin boat.

Chapter 22

THOSE TERRIFIC TOURISTS

A woman rushed into the Silver Trail Tourist Centre at Stewart Crossing, in Central Yukon, breathless with excitement. "We've just seen a musk ox up the road."

"But the musk ox range is five hundred miles North," I exclaimed.

"Well, we saw one. My husband has gone to borrow a gun. He wants it for his trophy room. Wish us luck." She bounded out the door, leaving me wondering how to save Simon Mervyn's Scotch Highland cow.

Here at the tourist centre, where I am manager, tables are sometimes turned on me and I am given more information than I give out. Such as the man from Florida who saw a snake slithering through the bushes. To my knowledge there hasn't been snake been seen in the Yukon since its sub-tropical forests were covered over by the great ice sheets of the Pleistocene period.

The Silver Trail starts on a geological phenomenon. Five hundred and sixty million years ago the Stewart Valley was a warm, shallow inland sea. Then great earth upheavals occurred, creating massive faults. The Tourist Centre sits almost on top of the Tintina fault, which is the collision point of the boundary plate between the North American continent and the Pacific plate.

The Centre itself is a unique building, planned and built by the genius of our local mining recorder, Roland Ronaghan. Because of its unusual design, it acts as a magnet for the tourists' cameras. When I hear the screech of brakes, I know the centre is going to have it's picture taken again. Since forty-two countries were registered at the centre, it's picture must now circle the globe.

Leaving the Silver Trail Centre at Stewart Crossing, the road crosses a bridge, bringing the tourists sharply up against a steep bluff and a decision. Here the road forks. Turn left and you head for the gold fields of the Klondike and Dawson City, with its honky-tonk entertainment, Diamond Tooth Gerty's Casino and crowds of sight-seeing tourists. Turn right and you're on the Silver Trail, which forms a loop through a vast, sparsely populated untamed wilderness, fulfilling a dream come true for many of Yukon's visitors, longing to experience nature alone at her best. The unusual unconformity of the Silver Trail gives outdoor lovers a chance to get acquainted with mother earth on his or her own. Here there is no entertainment to interrupt the appreciation of Nature's simplicity. In a sense, the trail is a test tube, measuring man's worth to himself and his beginnings.

A German tourist returning from his trip over the Silver Trail surprised me by quoting so appropriately from the great American naturalist, Enus Mills: "The trail compels you to know yourself and be yourself, and puts you in harmony with the universe. It makes you glad to be living. It gives health, hope, courage, and it extends that touch of nature which tends to make you kind. The trail is the most direct approach to the fountain of life, and in this immortal way delays age and commands youth to linger. When you delay along the trail, Father Time pauses to lean upon his scythe. The trail wanders away from the fever and fret, and leads to where the Red Gods call. This wonderful way must not be buried and forgotten."

Smiling happily, the German tourist said: "Enos Miles must have been writing about your Silver Trail."

"How did you ever find out about that wonderful naturalist?" I asked in surprise.

"Oh, we Germans have great love for nature, but we do not have the great outdoors like here, so we read about it, and if we are lucky, we come to see your wilderness." Before leaving, he shook my hand, smiling: "Your Silver Trail, makes one glad to be living."

A Texan standing nearby listening, asked: "Does your Silver Trail have any fishing?"

"Indeed there is good fishing. From Swan Lake, an Indian neighbor brought me a trout weighing forty six pounds."

"WOW! That's almost shark size, where can I find such a spot to fish?"

"Minto, Mayo and Ethel lakes can be reached by road and many excellent lakes by plane."

The Silver Trail is really a living library of the prehistoric past. Rocks and bones unravel for the interested geologist and zoologist a history dating back to the dawn of time. Here in the Stewart Valley once roamed vast herds of the largest mammals of the Pleistocene period. Woolly Mammoths fed along the edge of receding glaciers of Hungry Mountain, which can be seen from the tourist centre. A better view can be obtained at the turn out at mile KM 6. Here can be clearly seen the sharp line of dark green trees, the limit of Reid Glacier and the bare tundra top that escaped the glacier.

Twelve million years ago, there was a whole parade of pre-historic animals and reptiles. Marsupials, the saber toothed tigers, boa constrictor sized snakes, and Canes Dirus, or Dire Wolf, the six-foot tall wolf that was so terrible, the memory still lingers. The Elders of the Na-Cho Nyak Dun, the Mayo Indian band, have often warned me of this huge wolf when I was going into a remote area of the bush. Then there was the giant bison, Crassiocornis. Miners still find their skulls along the gold creeks.

Once I was asked: "Is there any chance of finding any prehistoric bone?"

"It has happened. A German couple was floating down the Stewart River from Mayo and found a mammoth toe bone being washed out of the bank, across from the old deserted Indian village."

An interesting collection of fossils can be seen at the museum in Keno City, which is at the top of the loop. It's a very old and quaint town. A man from California once enthused: "I thought I was driving onto a John Wayne movie set. When I saw the false front, crooked main street and cabins I expected the shooting to start any minute."

Another tourist vowed: "Seeing that old frontier town was the highlight of my trip."

The Silver Trail is a happy hunting ground for the rock hounds. Placer gold mines abound in Galena and other mineral and different rock specimens can be picked up around the silver mine. Keno Hill is one of the oldest silver mines on the continent, producing more millions in silver than did all the gold taken from the gold creeks of the famous Klondike.

Some of the miners are generous enough to let tourists pan for their own nuggets. Others, like the Gold Dusters, give unlimited panning time and serve refreshments for a small fee.

To the botanists, the Yukon in full bloom offers a challenge to find an undescribed, elusive species of plant. According to Wild Flower Guide, the excellent reference book published by the Alaska Northwest Publishing Co, there is always a strong possibility of finding an unknown flower in this Far Northern subarctic.

To the average tourist it comes as a surprise to see such lush plant growth when they had thought the Yukon was a land of perpetual ice and snow. We have miles of streams, bordered by the clear blue of wild for-get-me-nots. Hundreds of acres of Chiming Bells, their soft blues blending exquisitely with the pink wild roses and the magenta shades of the fireweeds.

It's a common belief that such profusion of plant life is due to the long day light hours. "Not so!" say scientists Peter Tomkins and Christopher Bird in their book The Secret Life of Plants. They say it's due to a special magnetic energy found in the Far North.

To the lovers of plants and flowers, the Silver Trail offers a fascinating treasure hunt.

Where once there were oddities of pre-historic animals living in the shadow of Hungry Mountain, a procession of pets now parades past the mountain. Dogs, cats, ferrets, white mice, monkeys, canaries, parakeets, hamsters, and even a bowl of gold fish, have been brought along for the ride. Judging by the majority of rotund shapes, the pets are over fed and too much loved to be left behind. At times they can and do create pandemonium. Like John, a big Irish Setter, who took off on his own to explore the Yukon. For hours we screamed and yelled "JOHN!" When his master was swearing that the next time John would be left at home, the dog showed up proudly dangling a snowshoe rabbit from his mouth. All was forgiven.

Then there was Skeeters, a mischievous Cocker Spaniel who raised havoc when he chased a tourist's cat across the picnic tables. Ham sandwiches, pickles, potato chips and pop flew all over the scenery.

Most tourists were so animated, being on their vacation, they wanted to share the epicurean delights they had brought with them. So I've eaten gourmet sausages from Germany, truffles from France, chocolates from Switzerland, cactus jelly from Arizona, pickled herring from Norway, pastas from Italy. A snake concoction from Florida was offered but I tactfully explained I was allergic to snakes. The tortilla from Mexico I swear burned out my tonsils with its pepper sauce, but their tequila was even worse. It made my eyes water and my nose run and it took some time before I could catch up with my breath.

One day trying to swat an annoying mosquito, a man from Sweden entered the Centre "You want no more mosquito bites?"

"I sure do."

He caught a mosquito, thrusting it at me. "Here eat it."

"What?"

"Eat it and all the other mosquitoes will be afraid of you because you are a mosquito cannibal." He wasn't kidding!

Reaction to the Yukon is as varied as the tourists. To so many the distances between settlements is overwhelming. One woman came into the Centre looking rather pale "Your country terrifies me. I can fancy a grizzly behind every tree."

Trying to reassure her I said "OH, I've lived here for several years and have only encountered seventeen grizzlies."

"SEVENTEEN!" she shrieked, "I'd die if I saw one."

The opposite reaction was demonstrated by a boy peddling his way across the North. He swaggered in and contemptuously demanded "Where's the bears?"

"You be careful," I warned "Bears aren't to be taken lightly."

"Oh, those garbage can rodents" he scoffed "I'd make quick work of them." From his pack he drew out a wide bladed knife about a foot long and drew it across his throat with strangled gurgle.

I had nothing to say in reply to his stupid ignorance. A trapper I knew twice the size of this boy had been killed by a grizzly when the only thing he had to fight with was a knife.

From a few tourists I've found out what the Yukon isn't. The Yukon is not a part of the United States of America. It does not belong to Alaska. In the winter Yukoners do not live in igloos. All the gold has not been found. Yukon Indians do not go on scalping parties.

Tourists come to the Yukon for many reasons. For adventure, for their health, for their honeymoon or just to prove they are brave enough to drive beyond the 60th parallel.

Most tourist problems are unexpected, and sometimes unbelievable. A woman from New York City came into the Centre laughing: "You won't believe this, but I got lost in Mayo."

"No, I can't believe it. Mayo has a population of about five hundred and one main street.

"Well, I did. Some poor old timer took pity on me and showed me how to get out of Mayo."

A San Francisco couple were surprised when they found themselves back in Dawson City, when they thought they would be in Whitehorse. Driving into a Government campground late at night, they simply went the wrong way when they drove out.

Anything that could run on wheels seemed to be the accepted vehicle to travel our highways, everything from huge, luxury motorhomes to bicycles. One of the most intriguing was a gypsy caravan, intricately carved and beautifully painted. Motorcycles seemed mostly driven by giant helmeted Germans dressed as if to invade Mars. However, it was the invasion of the Italians in their sixty jeeps that had the natives spellbound.

To the thousands of tourists who have traveled the Silver Trail I say: "Thanks for coming to the Yukon on your vacation. Come again because we think you are terrific."

Chapter 23

EDDY WILKENSEN DIED FIGHTING A GRIZZLY

(By Louis Brown)

My wife, Dolores, and I were holed up, during a -50°F cold spell in one of my old trapping cabins, making a pair of moose hide mitts, when we heard the local news from Whitehorse: "A Mayo trapper has been killed by a grizzly." It was the midwinter holiday season of 1977.

We know all the trappers in the area, and the eastern end of my trapline reaches almost to Mayo. We knew some of our friends would be worrying that it was one of us, as we were worrying about others.

I have been a trapper, a big game guide, and an outfitter ever since I came to the Yukon in 1934, and I have known of many men who, if not killed by grizzlies, have been badly mauled. I expect there would be more casualties if some "expert" advice were taken seriously. I've heard them say and seen them write: "Plant your feet firmly on the ground to meet a grizzly charge."

That can also plant you under the ground.

The radio crackled and the announcer said: "Brian Edwin Wilkensen, a long-time Yukon trapper, has been mauled and killed by a grizzly. The 58-year-old trapper had been trapping out from his Lansing River cabin, 120 miles east of Mayo. Returning from his own trapline cabin, about 30 miles down the Stewart River, his brother, Garret, found blood and pieces of clothing about 200 yards from the Lansing cabin. The frozen body of the grizzly was found a mile and a half beyond. Further details will be given after investigation by the Royal Canadian Mounted Police."

Dolores and I looked at each other, stunned. Eddy Wilkensen! How could it happen to Eddy? Eddy was born and raised on a trapline. He was probably the best-qualified man in the North to take care of himself in the bush. His near brushes with death in the northern wilderness were so phenomenal that he was nearly a legend.

Dolores burst into tears. "I've always hated Lansing. It's a terrible place." I had taken her there for our honeymoon. Rhubarb custard pie was her all-time favorite and at Lansing, rhubarb grows more than six feet high. But, after seeing the digging done by grizzlies around the old trading post, and their territorial marks on trees seven and eight feet above the ground, Dolores quickly lost her appetite for rhubarb pie.

Lansing is an old trading post, opened in 1905 by two partners known as Braine and Nash. A man named Farrel bought them out and, luckily, Farrel's wife was an excellent nurse. Christy, a trapper, shot a moose not far from the post and when he went back to get the meat a grizzly jumped him. Lonny Johnny, one of my old Indian guides, later told me that he had helped carry Christy in and described the terrible mauling the grizzly had given the trapper. He was only half alive when Mrs. Farrel started sewing him up. Because of her excellent nursing, Christy survived. Today there is a pass between the Yukon Territory and Northwest Territories named after him.

Soon after World War I, a flu epidemic wiped out most of the Indians in the area and Lansing post was abandoned. During the 1940s, Little Dave Moses and I trapped at Lansing for about seven years. There isn't a wilder country in the North.

Little Dave and I will readily admit that there were times when we were pretty scared. For one thing, the grizzlies in that area are large — the grizzlies in central and northern Yukon seem to be more aggressive and fiercer than those farther south. Old-timers used to speculate that those grizzlies had crossbred with the polar bear, thus inheriting all the cunning to track a man, the ability to hide and lie in wait, and a few other devilish traits possessed by the fearless and bold white bear. Over on the Wind and Bonnet Plume rivers, I've seen grizzly bears with white ruffs, white markings about the body, and some with all-white heads. I don't know whether this substantiates the old-timers' claim or not.

Little Dave and I were always on the alert. Grizzly signs were everywhere. Ralph Hampton, another trapper in the area, had his cabin in about the same place Garret has his, close to a few lakes. One spring in May, Little Dave and I headed down the Stewart River on our way to Mayo to replenish our supplies. We were surprised to see the dogs running loose along the bank when we reached Hampton's place. We stopped but no one was around. We were in a hurry, and almost left when we decided we had better take a look around. We found plenty of signs, all indicating that Hampton had run into trouble with a grizzly. We reported it to the RCMP. Hampton was never found.

Even during winter, Little Dave and I had to be on the lookout. Many of the big bears never hole up for the winter and the Indians are deathly afraid of a glaciered-out grizzly, and for good reason. They say a grizzly driven from his hole by a glacier not only is ravenously hungry, but he is usually coated with an armor of ice that an arrow can't penetrate. Before white men brought guns they had a rough time with such bears. Little Dave and I had plenty of close calls with grizzlies around Lansing.

Another thing that made it tough there were the large, aggressive wolf packs. We often wondered if there was a strain of Russian wolf in them, since so many were pure black.

Whenever Little Dave exclaimed, "that wolf not sound good," we'd drive our dog teams as fast as we could to a place where we could quickly start a fire. Little Dave is the proud grandson of Chief Johnson and the old man had sure schooled him in the way of the wolf.

Sometimes the packs were so large that they ate most of the game in a certain area, and then they would get hungry enough to eat their own droppings. We often came to large areas spattered with blood where they had been fighting and only a few patches of fur were left of their former pals.

That is the kind of country Eddy Wilkensen and his brother, Garret, moved to more than three years ago from the Pelly River area. I, too, had been trying to get the Lansing trapline again, but the two brothers beat me to it, much to Dolores's relief.

That fall (1975) when the Wilkensens moved to Lansing, Dolores began to worry about them, and it puzzled me that I kept having an uneasy feeling about them, too. After all, I told myself, Dave and I had survived there for seven years and no one was better conditioned for that kind of life than the Wilkensen brothers.

I heard rumors that they did run into some bad luck the first winter. Not being used to the country, they couldn't find moose and they had to shoot some of the dogs since there wasn't enough meat to feed them. Then Garret developed a double hernia and had a heck of a time getting out of the area that season. There were also reports of other things not going well.

Garret had been our watchman at home while we were away on our big game hunt. Several times, when the old Wilkensens still lived at Pelly Crossing, we had sat glued to our chairs watching home movies of Eddy and Garret driving their dog teams at breakneck speeds through the bush.

Eddy had so many close calls that I got to thinking of him as indestructible. Once his dad told me that Eddy had scared him half out of his wits when he came home and slumped against the door, dripping blood, with one eye almost put out. Eddy had shot a moose across a draw. He visually marked the place by a big dead tree and it took him some time to cross. He found the moose stretched out, looking dead. He leaned his gun against the dead tree, unsheathed his knife to cut the moose's throat when the moose leaped up and gored him. Eddy managed to thrash through the dead branches of the tree high enough to get out of the way of the maddened animal. He had to wait some time before the moose trotted away. It was a long hike home, and Eddy barely made it.

Another close shave came one spring when Eddy was trapping spring beaver at the head of Willow Creek. He was returning to camp with two beaver strapped on his packboard. The game trails were overgrown with thick willow clumps and suddenly, without warning, a grizzly charged out of the brush. Eddy barely had time to swing the rifle from his shoulder to snap a shot at the bear's head. Luckily, the bullet killed it instantly. Eddy found that what had so enraged the grizzly was that the bear had been eating on a moose calf nearby.

Another time Eddy was packing a Dall sheep off a mountain when a grizzly challenged his right to the carcass. Again, due to Eddy's lightning-fast action, the decision was made in Eddy's favour by a lucky snap shot.

Eddy had so many close calls that I was convinced he led a charmed life. The news of his death left me shocked. I left for Mayo to find out what I could.

My old guide, Lonny Johnny, told me that the RCMP had been to Lansing and had taken the coroner, Si Mason-Wood, with them. I went up to the Mining Recorder's office where Si was working and he gave me a few particulars.

The RCMP received the report of Eddy's disappearance two days after Christmas, 1977. Apparently, Garret had left Lansing for his own trapping cabin about 30 miles down river on November 29. He returned about two weeks later, expecting to find Eddy sitting in a warm, comfortable cabin. Instead, the older brother found a cold, dark, empty cabin. Eddy was nowhere to be found, and Garret started looking for him. Two hundred yards from the cabin Garret found wolf tracks, torn pieces of clothing and signs of blood frozen in the snow.

Still searching, Garret found the frozen carcass of the grizzly about a mile and a half down the river, but he could not find any sign of Eddy.

Garret then headed for his nearest neighbor, Peter Beattie, nearly 30 miles from Lansing. He asked Beattie to take his dog team into Mayo to inform the RCMP, then he returned alone to Lansing.

Apparently it took Beattie several days, as it was 120 miles of rough travelling in temperatures ranging between -50° and -60°. I could appreciate what a rough trip the man had, for I've covered the same trail many times.

One time in particular, Lonny Johnny and I were heading for Mayo to spend Christmas when a big bunch of wolves got on our trail. When Lonny, driving his team ahead of me, suddenly whipped up his dogs and drove like a thousand devils were after him I decided that if Lonny was in such a hurry I better get going, too. When we stopped on a point of an island where we had a good view of the river I yelled at him, "What in hell's wrong with you?" Lonny didn't take time to answer, but dashed to a spruce for some dry branches and not until the fire leaped to lick at the darkness of oncoming night did he tell me. "Bad bunch wolves; tell by his holler."

The wolves slunk around camp all night howling and moaning, as we fed the fire.

Garret had told the RCMP that about 200 yards from the cabin he and Eddy had traps set for marten, and whenever the dogs barked either he or Eddy would run out and take the marten out of the trap. After studying the tracks, it seemed that the dogs must have barked and Eddy had run out to check a trap; but it was evident the dogs had barked at the grizzly.

Si said: "We found where the bear had made his bed close by." No doubt the partly starved bear smelled food in the cabin and decided to hang around. Si wasn't exactly sure it was a bed the bear had used, and asked me, "Do bears really gather branches to make beds?"

I've often seen where grizzlies have made real comfortable beds under large spruce trees. Indians have told me they have seen grizzlies carrying spruce boughs in their arms, walking just like a man.

The grizzly must have just come into the area, for if Eddy had seen any sign of bear he certainly wouldn't have left his rifle in the cabin. He must have been in a hurry, too, since he was baking cookies and the book he was reading lay open on the table.

I kept thinking that if only he had a dog loose, it might have saved him. That is why in grizzly country I always keep a dog with me. I know from firsthand experience that my dogs have saved my life from grizzlies several times.

According to Mark Hoffman, of the Wildlife Branch, Eddy no doubt tried to defend himself with his knife. He said: "I suspect the grizzly may have been stabbed. Most trappers carry knives all the time. Eddy Wilkensen was the type of man who, in a confrontation, would resort to a knife even if it was a grizzly."

Eddy's body has never been found, but Si said they found where the grizzly buried something bloody and there were scraps of clothing and one small bone that looked like a finger or toe bone.

Later, talking to older Indians who are masters of the bush, I learned that it is their firm conviction that Eddy fought the grizzly with his knife, but was so badly mauled that he died. The grizzly, weakened by the stab wounds, could not travel any farther and died in his tracks. All signs indicated that a pack of wolves had finished the carnage.

Eddy Wilkensen was a born woodsman who never said an unkind word about any one. He was unique and incredible. His self-reliance, resourcefulness, fearlessness, and courage made him one of the last of the breed of the old-time mountain men.

Chapter 24

WOLVES AT MY DOOR

The Yukon is well known for it's temperature extremes but even the old sourdoughs were caught off guard when the mildness of early October changed to a wicked -35, during the latter part of the month.

The Arctic spruce stood stark and white under a thick layer of frost. A light snowfall was enough to cover the earth in a sparkling crystal carpet of deceptive tranquillity. Here in the Far North, life for both man and beast can be but a hair's breath from death.

In our sturdy log cabin, I was stirring a moose stew when I heard Kazan, our over sized Belgian Shepherd, barking in decibels that meant trouble. Grabbing the .270 Winchester from the gun rack, I hurriedly flipped up the folded-down open iron sights. Dashing to the cabin door and flinging it open, I glanced back at my husband. Louis had been lulled to sleep by the warmth of the old barrel stove after he had returned from a cold trip on his trapline. I hesitated a moment while I wondered if I should waken him in case I needed help.

Another uproar from Kazan and I dashed down the trail toward the corral. Several head of Scotch Highland cattle were peacefully chewing their cud, paying no attention to the blood chilling roars, snarls and howls coming from the thick brush behind them.

Before I could get the large pole gate open, Kazan and a grey wolf burst into the open, in a tangled ball of fighting fury. The cattle started milling and bawling, getting between the battling animals and me. Scrambling to the top of the gate, I tried to get a clear shot over the cattle, but before I could pull the trigger, a cow got her head in the sights. In desperation, I flopped to the frozen ground but now their legs were in the way. Snatching up a large stick, I flung it over the gate, yelling in octaves only panic can produce. A cow jumped to the side to avoid being hit. This opened a lane of fire and I screamed at Kazan. He jumped back giving me my one chance.

I pulled the trigger. The wolf gave a spasmodic jerk and went down but it was up the next moment, lunging for Kazan. The two rolled under the rail and tumbled among the cattle. The terrified cattle now raced in circles around the struggling pair, making it impossible to get in a shot. When I crawled between the bars in a frantic attempt to get the cattle behind me, my slick, seal-skin mukluks skidded on the frozen cattle urine and I fell flat on my face. This scared the cattle even more and, for a moment, they grouped at the far end of the corral. Firing from a belly position, I heard the bullet strike the wolf but the fighting didn't slow. Kazan appeared to be losing and looked badly hurt. The cattle started racing around. One of the cows didn't see me in time to detour so she jumped over me and one of her hind feet caught me in the side of the head, knocking off my parka hood. I screamed hoping to wake Louis. Kazan would surely be dead before I could get back to the cabin, if I went after help.

Kazan and I have had our wolf problems before. Living on a trapline in the Yukon you can always expect wolf problems, and I have learned to recognize and pay attention to my shepherd's wolf-warning barks because they're in a different key than his `company's coming' or `a husky is loose' barks. The only time I made the mistake of ignoring his wolf-warning barks, I ended up with every hair on my head feeling as if it was attached to one of Medusa's coils.

That day Kazan had killed two mother robins and was tied up in disgrace. As I passed him on the way to the cache, he was barking furiously. "Serves you right," I told him. "Stop trying to be a bird dog and you can be free."

As I drew close to the cache, Kazan seemed to go into hysterics. I rounded the log corner of the cache and ran into a wolf. Was the wolf surprised? It must have heard me coming. At that moment, I thought of nothing but retreat, but the wolf never moved. Gasping for breath I started to run and yell, "Wolf … WOLF!!!" Louis burst out of the cabin door carrying his .308 Savage.

"For God's sake, calm down," he said. "Where?" I didn't have to point, for the wolf was now in plain sight between the cache and the barn. Before Louis could get the sights on the wolf it was behind the barn, then out into the garden and crossing in front of us, only about 50 feet away. Louis shouldered his gun and followed its progress with the gun's .308 sight. I was about ready to collapse from the suspense. Why didn't my husband shoot? I couldn't stand it any longer and yelled "Shoot … SHOOT!"

"Hell, I can't," my husband exclaimed. "The tractor is right in line and I'm not going to blow a hole in my machinery for a lousy wolf."

I didn't buy that excuse. I think he was so mesmerized by the sheer audacity of the wolf that he forgot to shoot.

When Violet, a lovable husky, was let loose for a run and never came back we had our fears. Several nights later, Louis was sleeping in the tent by the trail, not far from the cabin, when Kazan awakened him with his familiar wolf bark. Taking his .308, Louis quietly eased through the tent flaps and sneaked a few paces up the trail. Between the branches of alder he saw movement. Looking through his 4X Lyman scope he saw a patch of fur about the size of a dollar. He doubted it would be possible to hit anything through so much brush but he made a snap shot. Louis could hardly believe his luck when he ran up the trail and found he had killed a large grey wolf. The next day my husband skinned him and opened him up to find some of poor Violet's hair inside.

Later, Cloudy, another husky, never returned from his run. When a husky doesn't return at chow time, it is very likely that he has ended up as an hors d'oeuvre for some wolf.

These dog and wolf skirmishes often have unexpected consequences. Old Silver Fox told about one of his huskies getting loose. The Indian followed the chain drag marks. Suddenly he came on his dog fighting a wolf. It was a matter of seconds before the wolf killed the husky and started dragging him off into the brush. Silver Fox ran back to his camp to get his gun. When he returned, he found the wolf lying beside the dog - dead.

We have a large cream-colored Siberian Husky named Sandy and he is hated with an unmitigated jealous passion by Kazan, who trounces him every chance he gets. Every night after losing a fight, Sandy — it seems in pure retaliation — jumps on top of his doghouse, raises his muzzle to the Northern skies and howls until he is answered by a long, drawn-out moan. If the moon is full and bright or the Northern Lights are strong, we can see the pack coming across the meadow. If it is a dark night, we switch on our Mini Venus 110,000-candlepower 12-volt spotlight. It is eerie seeing those gleaming yellow eyes. The doghouses are only 50 feet from our door but the close proximity of humans never stops the wolves. When they get close, Sandy sneaks into his doghouse leaving Kazan braced for a fight.

Louis has a strong opinion about this. "I know darn well Sandy does this to get the wolves in to lick Kazan."

We aren't always home to stop the fighting, so you can see that the fight in the corral I was first telling you about was just one more

173

battle for our shepherd. For once, it looked like he was getting the worst of it. I was frantic.

I knew quick action was needed but I didn't know where to place my next shot because the two bullets already in the wolf hadn't had much effect.

A young heifer drew too close to the fighting pair and was bitten. Bellowing and racing around the corral, she got the bull, Reigh Roary, Chieftain of Sequoia, upset and excited. He let out a roar, pawing and throwing shovels full of snow over his back until he looked like a snow blower. I jumped up, skidded to the fence, straddled the top pole, and yelled at the wolf, "I'll get you this time right in the head."

The open iron sights weaved back and forth on the combating pair. It was almost impossible to distinguish the grey head of the wolf from Kazan's darker coloring in their violent shifting of positions. When Kazan stumbled and fell, with the wolf right at his throat, I knew my pet would be dead anyway so I squeezed the trigger. When the bullet struck, the wolf's head flopped back. It lay still for a moment, then crawled under the fence. When I saw Kazan walk away alive I sank down on the snow trembling with relief that I hadn't killed him.

Louis came running toward me carrying his Winchester 30/30. "Are you trying to start a war?" he asked. "I think I killed a wolf," I told him. "What!? On my trapline? That's against the law," Louis said, blustering in mock seriousness, trying to kid me out of my state of agitation.

Louis walked over to the wolf and whistled. "He's a big one. I bet he'll weigh more than 175 pounds. But the fur auctioneer will sure dock us for those extra holes."

Kazan trotted over to give me a bloody but loving swipe across my cheek with his tongue. He was pretty well chewed up and one eye was closing fast, but he could still wag his tail. Seeing my pet torn and bleeding upset me. I snapped and said, "this place is hell."

"Never heard of hell being - 35°, " Louis replied, grinning and shivering in his shirtsleeves.

Over the years, I've written articles telling about wolves and their increasing predation of wildlife and domestic animals. I had hoped that sensible control, which would keep a balance between dwindling game populations and the growing wolf packs, would be established.

There was some action in Alaska, but people in the Yukon remained silent, with the exception of a few irate Whitehorse citizens who wrote letters informing me that wolves were on the endangered list, almost extinct and grossly misunderstood. Some correspondents were of the opinion that wolves should have priority over all other animals because of their romantic appeal to tourists, who provide valuable revenue to the Yukon.

Instead of counting sheep at night, I started counting the number of wolf packs I'd like to turn loose on the streets of Whitehorse. As it turned out, the wolves took care of the matter themselves. Metro-Goldwyn-Mayer couldn't have done a better job of scaring the wits out of people.

One recent fall we were astonished when we flipped the radio dial to the Canadian Broadcasting Corporation's Yukon News, to hear enraged farmers, who lived on the periphery of Whitehorse, telling of wolves ruthlessly killing their horses. One farmer stated that the predators had eaten thirty. The remaining horses were being kept in corrals for safety. This suited the wolves just fine because it was easier to jump the corrals fences to get their dinner than to chase the horses all over the landscape.

Like Alfred Hitchcock, the master of the thriller, the wolves didn't believe in letting the action slow. Louis and I stayed glued to our radio during local news time, not wanting to miss a single episode in this red-hot drama. We weren't disappointed because now the wolves went into high gear. The Yukon government's Department of Renewable Resources received a phone call from a person who said a wolf pack was ravaging downtown Whitehorse. The airwaves began to crackle with infuriated residents' descriptions of pet dogs being dragged from their doghouses and killed. The count of pets the wolves killed zoomed to ten, then twelve, and then fifteen. Moreover, this figure didn't include the dead cats, chickens, and pet rabbits.

Shirley Grant and Linda Beckett told of wolves coming within ten feet of their bedroom window and killing their two dogs. Grant angrily related how the wolf was large enough to be saddled and ridden by a nine-year-old child.

On hearing this, Louis shook his head and told me: "The department of tourism must be feeding the wolves vitamin supplements to make them bigger to attract the tourists."

Later, the Yukon News ran a picture of Grant and Beckett riding shotgun at their residence. The distraught Grant said: "If nothing else. I'll have the satisfaction of shooting my dog's killer."

Now the press became alarmed and was of the opinion that:

"Anything that moves is a threat. It could be someone else's family pet or it could be a child or an adult out for an evening stroll."

Louis agreed and warned me. "You'd better not wear your wolf cap to Whitehorse anymore. You'll get plugged for sure."

Grant told the press: "I know they (conservation officers) can't bring back my dogs, but I wish they would at least make more of an effort to get the wolves."

On hearing this I could hardly believe my ears, remembering those scathing letters I had received from Whitehorse residents and their pleas to save the wolves at all costs.

Grant also revealed that one officer had admitted that a wolf could attack a child if it were hungry enough. She said: "It scares the hell out of you."

I fully sympathized with the two women, but I doubted any wolf would be dumb enough to make himself a target just to appease them. If the action slowed down, the wolves ate another pet dog or cat to rekindle the uproar. As if to taunt Whitehorse residents, the wolves would howl back at the one-time wolf lovers who admitted they were terrified. Sometimes I couldn't help smiling. The wolves were doing an excellent job of proving they weren't extinct.

But the big shocker came when Horst Mueller, a Whitehorse resident, sizzled the airwaves when he reported that his mother, who lived in West Germany, had called to make sure her grandchildren were safe. She told him that Bild Zeitung, one of Europe's largest newspapers with a circulation of nearly six million, had published a story telling of children in Whitehorse being devoured by wolves and of seven northern Canadians being killed by wolves.

Not only was the Bild Zeitung having a field day with sensational stories, so was England's Daily Mirror. Our own Yukon News grew alarmed and ran a headline: "Wolf Story In Paper Could Mean Disaster For Tourism."

Howard Tracey, the Minister of Renewable Resources, said in an interview that his primary concern about the European accounts was that they could damage tourist travel to the Yukon.

The wolves were getting too high a rating to just remain on the local CBC news. They were becoming celebrities and reaching stardom fast. Now they began to be featured on CBC coast-to-coast radio shows such as Sunday Morning, Morning Side and As It Happens. Listening to the CBC's top commentators talking about our Yukon wolves made us think our predators had reached the top of the ladder of fame but we were wrong.

Next thing we knew, they were crowding celebrities off the screen. On January 13, 1983, The Journal television show presented the wolves. We now expect Hollywood to give our wolves an Oscar for the best performance of the year.

At long last, the Yukon government announced that a $50,000 wolf-management program would be launched. The program was designed to create an economic incentive for trappers to catch wolves. Each trapper is to receive $200 for every wolf pelt turned over to the department of renewable resources for auction.

At a recent birthday celebration, I raised my glass high to give a toast: "Here's to wolves," I said, "God bless them. They induced the Yukon into action when I couldn't." Just the other day, the Yukon News raised the question: "Where will it end?" Knowing wolves and how few are stupid enough to get into a trap, I'd say it's just beginning.

Chapter 25

YULETIDE IN THE YUKON

Christmas in the Northern bush offers a wonderful way to celebrate the Savior's birth with Mother Nature. Here the billowing aurora borealis is more spectacular than any city's garish window display. Here the singing of wolves falls louder on the midnight air than a church choir. Here it's more exciting to watch a live willow grouse in the poplar trees than to just sing about a partridge in a pear tree. Here our Yukon moose could out run Rudolph on any snowy trail. Best of all, you don't have to pray for little white crystals to pad the skies on Santa's sleigh, because here old Santa can deliver presents for seven months of the year.

Most people think the true spirit of Christmas is the coming together of family. It's the same in the Yukon's wilderness, except our family is furred and feathered. The wildlife have their own Christmas tree beside our log cabin home. The tree skirt is of wild timothy hay for the snow shoe rabbits. The top branches are gobbed with peanut butter for the squirrels and other chattering, frisky creatures. The middle branches are hung with moose fat rolled in lamb quarter and seeds for the Boreal Chickadees, Grey Jay and Downy Woodpeckers. If we are lucky, the Rose Breasted Grosbeaks, like animated ornaments, give colorful, bright trim to the tree. The lower branches are tied with meaty bones and gaily wrapped packages for the huskies.

Once, we brought all the huskies together to the tree for the singing of carols on Christmas Eve. In full voice, Louis and I were struggling to harmonize on our favorite carol and loudly vocalizing Peace on Earth, when a violent dispute erupted over the bones. After that, to maintain the peaceful spirit of Christmas, each husky has his turn at the tree. It almost breaks me up to see their big brown eyes pleading to hurry and give the signal so they can open their packages. Once given, paper and ribbons explode and there is as much smacking over the cracklings as I do over a box of Halvah.

178

For the cabin, three trees must be decorated. A tiny one for the doll house, a ceiling high blue spruce for the window corner, and the potted Norfolk pine that always seems to say "me too".

Somehow, the garish glitter of the traditional Christmas tree trims seemed too flagrant for the solidity and tranquillity of the Yukon. It's a young land, a land of new beginnings where new traditions are in the making. I wanted to improvise a new tradition for decorating our very own first Christmas tree. Trims that not only would express the Christmas spirit, but also the true spirit of the Yukon.

Deciding the new traditional Christmas tree must represent everything wonderful about the Yukon, I rolled up my sleeves without the least idea as to how it was going to be accomplished. Browsing through grandmother's old cookbook produced an idea. Pink, yellow and lavender, would give the effect I was seeking. It took half of our winter sugar supply before I could get the sugar to spin. Once the trick was learned, to drip the hot syrup over to wooden spoons, my mukluks were wading in spun sugar.

No cookie cutters of the right design existed, so I had to originate master patterns on cardboard, place them on gingerbread cookie dough, and laboriously cut around them. They were lightly browned in the oven, then cooled, frosted and highlighted with white powdered sugar and melted dark chocolate.

While working on the trims, I decided the Yukon must have its own traditional poem. Not being an Edna St. Vincent Mallay, I doubted my ability to soar to her ethereal heights of poetry. Perhaps Ogden Nash would be more my style? Rhyming words began to bubble in my brain. When Louis came in with an armload of wood, I desperately asked, "what will rhyme with itching?"

"Don't ask me to help you with that blasted poem. An hour ago you asked me what would rhyme with fight and I almost sawed off my leg with the power saw because I was trying to think of a word that would. Why not have the Shooting of Dan McGrew, and be done with it? That's Yukonish enough."

"Shooting McGrew, on Christmas? NEVER! Christmas is Peace on Earth. Remember?

"Tell that to the rest of the world. They don't seem to stop shooting long enough to find out."

The summer before I had searched for the whitest caribou moss I could find. Now I strung the lacy plant into long ropes. Finished the rest of the trims, I strapped on my snowshoes and yelled for Louis.

"Let's go get our Christmas tree" Hopefully we could find one that would do justice to the trimmings I had worked so hard to make the new tradition original.

"Be with you as soon as I find the axe," Louis answered.

As usual, the bright orange prospector's tape we had used the previous summer to mark the perfect tree couldn't be found under the heavy snowfall of last week. Like a very large string of beads, the tracks of a lynx lead into thick timber and we followed. Suddenly, the snow seemed to explode in front of us as grouse flew from their cozy hideouts under the snowdrifts. As we tapped snow from the trees, squirrels scolded us for disturbing their winter nap. Deep in the woods, an owl hooted. Now I knew what was going to displace the angel on the tip of the tree.

A pack of wolves serenading from a distant ridge jerked my thoughts back from visions of what Santa might be giving me. Northern Lights started flaring up from the darkening horizon. Icy stars winked into twinkling lights one by one and I wondered if the star of Bethlehem was among them.

Louis warned: "You better decide fast as I expect the temperature to drop below 0 by morning."

"This one has lots of bushy branches and cones but it's too tall."

"Easy to cut down in size," Louis said, swinging the axe. As it swayed, I stood ready to grab it before it crashed to save the frozen branches from snapping off.

We were half way to the cabin before we noticed a wolf trotting on the river ice below us. Glancing up now and then, he seemed to be curious over the travelling tree. When the cabin was in sight, he took off and disappeared into the Northern night.

The tree trimming had to wait until morning because my snowshoe muscles were screaming for me to get off of them so they could relax. Creating my masterpiece of Christmas ingenuity had deflated my dynamic enthusiasm to exhaustion. I decided there was only one thing that could revive me. A big hunk of Christmas fruit cake.

The recipe for it was given to me by Bud Fisher, whose white whiskers bordering a cherry-cheeked grin make him a perfect replica of the jolly old elf. Bud had filched it from a 1956 Ladies Home Journal and had renamed it, The Traditional Yukon Fruit Cake. He sponsored its popularity by baking dozens and sharing with his fellow Yukoners. It's so delicious, I risked my life to get the recipe and share with you.

Bud's Traditional Yukon Fruit Cake

2 cups whole Brazil nuts
1½ cups whole red maraschino cherries
1½ cups candied pineapple diced
½ lb dates, pitted

Sift the following over the top four items:
¾ cup flour,
½ tsp baking powder
½ tsp salt

Mix above until coated.
Beat *three eggs* foamy, add *1 tsp vanilla*, pour over mixture.
Turn into a foil lined 9" x 5" x 3" pan.
Bake in slow oven for one hour and forty-five minutes.
When cool, wrap in a rum-soaked cloth and let mellow
   for a few weeks.

Once, a grizzly thought it totally unnecessary for it to mellow. To avoid a last minute Christmas rush, a Yukon woman decided to bake her fruit cake a couple of months before the holiday season. She then went for a short trip. While she was away from home, a grizzly sauntering by, sniffed the air and caught a tantalizing whiff of a promising snack. Tearing the door off the hinges, ripping open the refrigerator, deep freeze and cupboards, his efforts were finally rewarded with the best tasting grub he had ever eaten. Unmellowed, the Christmas cake was devoured to the last crumb.

After the fourth piece of fruitcake, I revived enough to think about trimming the tree. Could I have had another piece, I'm sure it would have enervated me enough to have completed the masterpiece of new tradition, but Louis had come in with spruce boughs, snatched the cake plate away with a grin, and wolfed it down with glee.

That night instead of counting sheep, I tried to rhyme words. My poetical inspiration had jammed. I wondered if Elizabeth Browning had ever come to such a blank wall. Instead, she would have written beautiful poems about the Northern Lights seen through the window, billowing and waving in glorious shades of pinks, greens, yellows and lavenders.

Not until morning did I muster enough energy to trim the tree. Twining the ropes of caribou moss among the soft needled bright green branches, I then made swags of pink, green and yellow spun sugar and draped them between the branches. Along the white trails of moss marched antlered migration of caribou in their white icing capes. Chocolate frosted moose yarded on the lower branches, while powdered sugar Dall sheep grazed peacefully near the top on spruce cones. Fierce cocoa-coated grizzlies prowled everywhere. Here and there candied Canadian Honkers and one lone Sand Hill crane froze in flight. Clumps of cherry red, low bush cranberries gave a gay dash of color. The gauzy hues of the spun sugar Northern lights gave a unique beauty. The guardian of this Northern scene was a seal skin owl clinging to the tip of the tree.

I was busy frying moose steaks when Louis came in, shaking the new fallen snow from his parka. Bursting with excitement I told him "dear, hurry and go look at the tree". I was expecting "Oos" and "Ahs" and was unprepared for his deplorable comment.

"Not a good trophy head in the bunch and it looks like they ran into a pack of wolves."

"What are you talking about?"

"Well that moose lost his head and the rear end of that caribou is gone and…"

"WHAT!!!" I yelled and like a shot raced over to the tree because when the wild game of ginger bread were hung, they all had their heads and rear ends.

"PUNKY" I shouted. A ten-pound poodle of questionable ancestry tried to sneak further under the tree. I pulled him out with a half a sticky furred grizzly sticking out of his mouth.

The next day I was feeling sorry, no one else would see my new traditional mastership of the Yukon's spirit of Christmas, when Louis laughingly told me. "Oh, your tree was admired alright. Last night a big lynx sat under the window admiring it for so long he melted the snow to the ground.

Christmas Eve came and we started our program with Nelson Eddy, singing White Christmas. Next, Louis told how a wolverine once stole his Christmas dinner, then Punky did his favorite trick rolls, which were suppose to leave his audience spellbound. Suddenly Louis jumped up, made a very exaggerated bow, and announced: "It gives me great pleasure to introduce to you Yukon's Poet Laureate, who will recite for the first time ever, Yukon's treasured traditional Christmas poem."

Struggling to match Louis's solemnity, I cleared my throat:

Twas the night before Christmas, when NOT in the house,
The huskies were howling, the dead to arouse.
The moose meat was hung by the stovepipe with care,
In hopes that a wolverine would never come there.
My wife in her woolies and I in my Stanfield itching,
To bed with the sourdough starter to keep it from freezing.
When out in the zero'd air there arose such commotion.
I fell over the stove wood, without any notion,
Tore open the door, threw out the cat,
To find that a grizzly was climbing the cache,
"My fruit cake," she shrieked, "I stored for to mellow."
My knees started shaking like two lumps of jelly,
To the top of the ladder, he growled not a thing,
His breath wreathed his head like the crown of a king.
His fur gleamed all silver in the frosty moonlight.
He looked like Jack Dempsey, just itch'n to fight
His eyes, how they glared, his snout began sniffing,
The rum in the fruitcake started him twitching.
As spry as old Santa and as quick as a flash,
He slurped up the fruit cake, then made a fast dash,
But stopping and turning, to Walt Disney's delight,
He burped:
"Merry Christmas from the Yukon and to all a good-night."

MORE GREAT BIOGRAPHIES

Afloat in Time
Jim Sirois
ISBN 0-88839-455-1
5.5 x 8.5 • sc • 288 pp

Alaska Calls
Virginia Neeley
ISBN 0-88839-970-7
8.5 x 11 • sc • 208 pp.

**Beyond the
Northern Lights**
W.H. Bell
ISBN 0-88839-432-2
5.5 x 8.5 • sc • 288 pp.

Bootleggers Lady
Sager/Frye
ISBN 0-88839-976-6
5.5 x 8.5 • sc • 286 pp.

Bush & Arctic Pilot
Al Williams
ISBN 0-88839-433-0
5.5 x 8.5 • sc • 256 pp.

**Captain McNeil & His
Wife the Nishga Chief**
Robin Percival Smith
ISBN 0-88839-472-1
5.5 x 8.5 • sc • 256 pp.

Chilcotin Diary
Will D. Jenkins Sr.
ISBN 0-88839-409-6
5.5 x 8.5 • sc • 272 pp.

**Crazy Cooks &
Gold Miners**
Joyce Yardley
ISBN 0-88839-294-X
5.5 x 8.5 • sc • 224 pp.

Curse of Gold
Elizabeth Hawkins
ISBN 0-88839-281-8
5.5 x 8.5 • sc • 288 pp.

Descent into Madness
Vernon Frolick
hc • 0-88839-300-8
sc • 0-88839-321-0
5.5 x 8.5 • 368 pp.

Fogswamp
Turner/McVeigh
ISBN 0-88839-104-8
5.5 x 8.5 • sc • 255 pp.

**Gang Ranch:
The Real Story**
Judy Alsager
ISBN 0-88839-275-3
8.5 x 11 • sc • 288 pp.

**The Incredible
Gang Ranch**
Dale Alsager
ISBN 0-88839-211-7
5.5 x 8.5 • sc • 448 pp.

Klondike Paradise
C.R. Porter
ISBN 0-88839-402-0
8.5 x 11 • sc • 176 pp.

Lady Rancher
Gertrude Rogers
ISBN 0-88839-099-8
5.5 x 8.5 • sc • 184 pp.

Nahanni Trailhead
Joanne Ronan Moore
ISBN 0-88839-464-0
5.5 x 8.5 • sc • 256 pp.

Puffin Cove
Neil Carey
ISBN 0-88839-216-8
5.5 x 8.5 • sc • 178 pp.

Ralph Edwards
Ed Gould
ISBN 0-88839-100-5
5.5 x 8.5 • sc • 296 pp.

Real Alaskans
Lewis Freedman
ISBN 0-88839-254-0
5.5 x 8.5 • sc • 224 pp.

**Ruffles on my
Longjohns**
Isobell Edwards
ISBN 0-88839-102-1
5.5 x 8.5 • sc • 297 pp.

**Wheels, Skis
and Floats**
Burton/Grant
ISBN 0-88839-428-4
5.5 x 8.5 • sc • 172 pp.

**Where Mountains
Touch Heaven**
Ena Powell
ISBN 0-88839-365-2
5.5 x 8.5 • sc • 222 pp.

Wild Trails, Wild Tails
Bernard McKay
ISBN 0-88839-395-4
5.5 x 8.5 • sc • 176 pp.

Wings of the North
Vera Turner
ISBN 0-88839-060-2
5.5 x 8.5 • sc • 288 pp.

Yukon Lady
Hugh Maclean
ISBN 0-88839-186-2
5.5 x 8.5 • sc • 192 pp.

**Yukon Riverboat
Days**
Joyce Yardley
ISBN 0-88839-386-5
5.5 x 8.5 • sc • 176 pp.

Yukoners: True Tales
H. Gordon-Cooper
ISBN 0-88839-232-X
5.5 x 8.5 • sc • 144 pp.

from HANCOCK HOUSE publishing